"Award-winning author Jane Cle[...]
and entertaining page-turner abc[...]
tering Suspense, Structure, & Plot [...]
—Wendy Corsi Staub, New York T[...]

"Unputdownably indispensable! For newbie authors and veterans alike, this terrific how-to is your new go-to. Don't write your book without it—it's a treasure." —Hank Phillippi Ryan, Agatha, Anthony, Macavity and Mary Higgins Clark award-winning author

"Masterful! I love this book. Oh, how I wish I'd had it when I was struggling with my first crime novel. This is a gold mine of information, of insight on how to structure and pace the novel. Brilliant. And even as I write my current book, I find myself reflecting on her insights and using them. This isn't about being formulaic. It's about first understanding the structure, and then making it your own. *Mastering Suspense, Structure, & Plot* is an absolutely extraordinary resource for anyone serious about writing not just a crime novel, but any book." —Louise Penny, #1 *New York Times* best-selling author

"Jane Cleland had drawn a detailed road map for navigating the suspense-writing journey. In a well-thought-out and artfully constructed way, she concisely covers it all. I wish I had read *Mastering Suspense, Structure, & Plot* before I ever started writing mysteries, but I sure am glad to have this book now." —Mary Jane Clark, *New York Times* best-selling author

"Leave it to Jane Cleland, the reigning queen of the traditional mystery, to reveal the secrets of suspense—and to take the sweat out of writing today's hottest genre!"—Paula Munier, senior literary agent at Talcott Notch Literary Agency and author of *Plot Perfect*

MASTERING

SUSPENSE STRUCTURE & PLOT

JANE K. CLELAND

WRITER'S DIGEST
BOOKS

Writer's Digest Books
An imprint of Penguin Random House LLC
penguinrandomhouse.com

Printed in the United States of America

ISBN 978-1-59963-967-3

Edited by Chelsea Henshey
Designed by Alexis Estoye

ABOUT THE AUTHOR

Jane K. Cleland writes the multiple award-winning Josie Prescott Antiques Mystery series (St. Martin's Minotaur), which is often reviewed as an *Antiques Roadshow* for mystery fans. Library Journal named the first in the series, *Consigned to Death*, a "core title" for librarians looking to build a cozy collection, one of only twenty-two titles listed, along with books by Agatha Christie and Dorothy L. Sayers. "Josie" stories have also appeared in *Alfred Hitchcock Mystery Magazine*. In addition, Jane has published four nonfiction books.

Jane chairs the Black Orchid Novella Award, one of the Wolfe Pack's literary awards, granted in partnership with *Alfred Hitchcock Mystery Magazine*. She is a past chapter president of the Mystery Writers of America, New York Chapter, and served on the national board. Additionally, Jane is the host of the Writer's Room, a series of interviews with authors and industry professionals that appears on cable television and online (BronxNet).

Jane has both an MFA (in professional and creative writing) and an MBA (in marketing and management). She's a member of the full-time faculty of Lehman College, part of the City University of New York (CUNY) system, where she is also the Director of the Program for Professional Communications. She also mentors MFA students in the Western Connecticut State University MFA in Creative and Professional Writing Program and facilitates writing workshops, including Aspiring Writer's Weekend and Memoir Writing, both sponsored by MIT/Endicott House.

In addition, Jane is a frequent guest author at university writing programs, a featured presenter at major writing conferences, a much-loved facilitator at writing workshops, and a popular speaker at library and corporate events.

DEDICATION

This is for Ruth Chessman, my mother.

And of course, for Joe.

ACKNOWLEDGMENTS

Thank you to the Writer's Digest team for their insights and guidance, especially those with whom I have worked most closely: publisher Phil Sexton, managing editor Rachel Randall, associate editor Chelsea Henshey, designer Alexis Estoye, copyeditor Kim Cantanzarite, and proofreader Betsy Ballenger.

I also want to acknowledge my fiction editors: executive editor Hope Dellon and associate editor Silissa Kenney from St. Martin's Minotaur, and editor-in-chief Linda Landrigan from *Alfred Hitchcock Mystery Magazine*. Special thanks go to my literary agent Cristina Concepcion.

I also want to thank Paula Munier for suggesting that I write this book, Jean Galiana who encouraged me to tell my mother's stories, G. D. Peters for his insights as to which examples I should include, and all the authors whose work has inspired me.

TABLE OF CONTENTS

PART ONE
THINKING

PART TWO
WRITING

FOREWORD

Like so many writers, my earliest efforts were memoir. I took episodes from my life and wrote them down. There was the time I hitchhiked and the driver of the Cadillac that picked me up lectured me in graphic detail about what could happen if I ended up in the wrong car. The time I nearly killed my sister by tying her tricycle to my two-wheeler so she could go faster.

Like the bike and the trike, I strung the episodes together, thinking that I was writing a book, and though the sentences were perfectly nice, the paragraphs eminently readable, and sometimes I even made myself laugh, I'd read enough good literature to know that the incidents were banal and disconnected and the characters were cardboard. Worst of all, my "story" had no shape.

I thought I could write a book because I'd been reading books for years. But all I'd done was open a vein and let the words flow. Turns out that a series of episodes is not the same as a storyline or plot.

Which led to my first epiphany: Writing a book is a lot harder than it looks. Boy, do I wish I'd had Jane K. Cleland's wonderful book to refer to back then. Learning that structure really is "king" (see chapter two) would have helped me shape my episodic narrative into a cohesive whole.

As I continued to work on that still unpublished manuscript, I experienced many more writing epiphanies, including this one: It's easier to start a book than it is to finish it, particularly if you want the ending to feel earned and satisfying (see Jane's "Triple X Strategy").

It took me a long time and many rejections to learn what readers discover in *Mastering Suspense, Structure, & Plot*. A novel needs a story arc and its characters need trajectories, and I desperately needed "Jane's Plotting Road Map," which you'll find in chapter three.

Jane's advice, like "isolate your protagonist," has me tightening my suspense and amping the forward momentum of my own work in progress. She's given me a new appreciation for red herrings, taking them far beyond mere plot devices. And should my writing gears get stuck from a surfeit of structure, she's got advice for dealing with "analysis paralysis."

Even after nine novels, I still struggle with plot and structure. Flying by the seat of my pants, I invariably end up creeping forward and endlessly circling back to second-guess myself. Though I'm always happy with the result, it's a long ugly process that Jane's techniques streamline. Her focus on story structure, plot, and suspense promise to get me there in much less time with much less mess.

In short, you could write a book about what I needed to know about writing a book, and Jane has done just that. *Mastering Suspense, Structure, & Plot* is chock full of tips and techniques, insights, and wise advice. She's anything but dogmatic, saying to writers "try this and see if it works for you." She illustrates her points with examples drawn from the full range of storytelling genres, from classic literature to modern romance and from memoir to thriller. Clever exercises put her ideas into practice. Her suggestions are both practical and smart.

My tiny office has limited shelf space, but this book I'll keep and refer to again and again. It's a book that should be on every writer's desk.

HALLIE EPHRON is the *New York Times* best-selling author of *Night Night, Sleep Tight* and eight other suspense novels. Her novel, *Never Tell a Lie*, was made into Lifetime Movie Network movie. Her books have been finalists for Edgar, Anthony, and Mary Higgins Clark awards, and she is an award-winning book reviewer for *The Boston Globe*.

INTRODUCTION

> Writing has laws of perspective, of light and shade just as painting does, or music. If you are born knowing them, fine. If not, learn them. Then rearrange the rules to suit yourself.
>
> —TRUMAN CAPOTE

When I was in my midtwenties and my mother was in her late sixties, she called me at work. I was the business manager of a nonprofit, deep in a month-end reconciliation.

"I need to see you," she said. "It's urgent."

I grabbed my purse and ran for the door, pausing only to poke my head into my boss's office to tell him that I had to go, that I had a family emergency. He nodded gravely and asked me to keep him posted, and to let him know if there was anything he could do.

If you're like most people, you want to know what happened. When your readers know something is happening, or might happen, to characters they care about, but they don't know what it is—that's the foundation of suspense. How you set it up, how you structure it, how you develop it as a story, and how you reveal it is the craft of writing. Those are the subjects of this book.

My mother sat in frozen silence, tears streaming down her cheeks, a ripped and crumpled envelope resting on her lap.

I walked slowly toward her. "What's happened?"

She handed me the envelope, her lips quivering.

I extracted the letter and read it, then read it through a second time. I raised my eyes to her face.

"Oh, Ma," I said.

Suspense doesn't have to involve high-speed car chases or eerily shaped shadows flitting outside the window. It is inherent in the kinds of real incidents that happen to real people. Regardless of your chosen genre, it's your job to cull the suspenseful from the prosaic, and this book will show you how.

Part One of this book guides your thinking as you develop your plot or story plan and create a structure that sets an appropriate pace. Part Two explains specific writing techniques to ratchet up the tension and increase suspense. Dozens of examples from best-selling authors demonstrate how to integrate suspense into your overarching structure and plot or story plan. Exercises ensure you can apply the principles. Additionally, two case studies will document a reliable process to develop a can't-put-it-down plot or story.

In one case study, a frightening everyday incident (a purse stolen from a grocery cart) plunges the protagonist into a terrifying nightmare (a domestic thriller); in the other, a man juggling multiple and conflicting priorities (his aging father, rebellious child, demanding career, and impatient wife) struggles to find balance in his life (narrative nonfiction). These case studies highlight the real-world practicality and usability of every tip, tool, and technique discussed in this book.

Evidently, my sixty-six-year-old mother wanted to become a psychotherapist. Unbeknownst to me, she'd applied to a master's program that offered a specialized degree—and she got in.

"You didn't tell me you applied," I said.

"I didn't tell anyone. I didn't want to jinx myself."

I grinned. "You're some hot mama."

She brushed the wetness from her cheeks. "Can you believe I got in?"

"Yes."

"I'm sorry I called you away from work, but I just had to tell you in person."

I knelt before her, placed the letter on the carpet and smoothed it out, then grasped her hands. "I think we should make a rule. Every time you get into grad school, you should call me away from work."

She hugged me then, and I hugged her back, and all I could think was that I hoped every family emergency I'd ever face ended like this.

Suspense is the heart and soul of storytelling. Without suspense, the only readers who will persevere are those who are keenly interested in your topic. To keep your readers engaged, you need to tell a gripping story that involves relatable characters. If the incidents are boring, banal, or contrived; if the pace is slow or erratic; or if readers can't connect with the people you're writing about, they will lose interest. By the end of this book, you'll be crafting stories readers can't put down. Those are the stories readers love. Those are the stories that sell.

PART ONE

THINKING

CHAPTER ONE

KNOW YOUR READERS

> **"** I've learned that people will forget what you said, people will forget what you did, but people will never forget how you made them feel. **"**
>
> —MAYA ANGELOU

WRITE FOR YOUR READERS

Shortly after I submitted the manuscript for *Antiques to Die For*, the third entry in my Josie Prescott Antiques Mystery series, my St. Martin's Minotaur editor took me to lunch. She'd barely sat down before she said, "I realized overnight what the problem is—you don't know you're writing cozies."

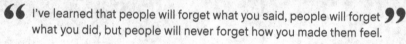

COZY MYSTERIES DEFINED

The term *cozy*, a subgenre of traditional mysteries (which is itself a subgenre of crime fiction), derives from a tea cozy, the charming, usually hand-sewn or -crocheted teapot cover designed to keep the

MASTERING SUSPENSE, STRUCTURE, & PLOT

contents warm. The name is a nod to the genre's creator, Agatha Christie. One of Ms. Christie's most famous detectives, Miss Marple, rarely left her English country village, relying not on forensics, but on her knowledge of human nature to solve crimes. (See Figure 1.1 for a list of elements and attributes common to traditional mysteries, including cozies.) While some contemporary cozies stretch the limits of credibility (cats solving the crimes, for instance), many are quite literary in tone, even erudite.

This was, by the way, the first I heard there was a problem. I was, needless to say, shocked, chagrined, and appalled. An hour later, I had a different view. I was still shocked, chagrined, and appalled, but only with myself. I had lost sight of my readers. I was going through a hard time, and I had allowed my emotional turmoil to infiltrate my novel. Instead of writing sweet, I wrote dark. My readers love my books because they're predictable. Not the stories, of course, but the ensemble cast and small-town location don't change, and the underlying principles of fair play, honesty, and goodness are woven into every story. By adding elements more appropriate to a noir novel, like angry confrontations between my protagonist, Josie, and her boyfriend, Ty, I risked alienating my readers.

An important point is that I never thought of myself as a cozy writer before that seminal lunch. I didn't know my genre and I didn't know my readers. Since that day, I've worked hard to honor my readers by creating intricate, surprising plots, all set in the charming small coastal town of Rocky Point, New Hampshire. While my characters grow and face unexpected challenges, the feel of my stories is comfortable and comforting. To my readers, picking up a Josie story is like putting on a favorite old sweater.

I have always been grateful that my editor took the time to explain what I was doing wrong. She could have simply rejected the manuscript. Instead she gave me the opportunity to fix it. She helped me understand what makes my novels "good."

Determining whether a story is "good," is, of course, subjective, but there are two features that most published books share. First, they're simultaneously fresh and familiar. This dual expectation seems oxymoronic, but it isn't. From a publisher's perspective, if a work isn't fresh, why bother publishing it? Yet, if it isn't familiar, that same publisher won't think he knows how to market it. For instance, when thriller fans pick up a book, they look forward to a specific reading experience—they want to root for a hero who will save the day against increasingly complex and dangerous odds. That's the basic structure of a thriller. Yet if the novel features characters readers have met before or if your characters face challenges readers have seen before, the story will fall flat. Why would a publisher back a novel that feels derivative? Why would a reader buy it? To succeed, your stories need to meet genre expectations while surprising readers. The trick is to layer the unexpected onto the familiar.

The second feature that most published books share is something in the writing that touches readers' hearts and makes them feel the characters' yearnings. To achieve that level of reader connection requires a deep understanding of what makes your readers tick.

Some authors will disagree with this reader-centric mind-set. These authors write what they want to write, believing if they do it well, their books will find an audience. That works sometimes, and I don't mean to disdain that process out of hand. I never argue with success, and all writers have to find their own path to publication. For me, however, using such a freewheeling method is counterproductive. If I lose sight of my readers and write a book that doesn't get read, it's like cooking a bang-up dinner no one eats. I want my readers to have confidence that if they buy my book, they will get the reading experience they expect.

Q: Writing for readers sounds like pandering to me.

A: *Pander* is a strong word, and if it feels like you're prostituting yourself, then obviously you shouldn't do it. In the foreword to *"I Gotta Tell You"* (edited by Matthew Seeger), the great orator and business turnaround expert, Lee Iacocca, wrote, "I've been asked many times what makes a good speech. Good writing, practice, something worthwhile to say—all of them are important. But I think that if a speaker begins with a deep sense of obligation to the audience, everything else falls into place." Iacocca's sense of duty translates perfectly to the pact authors should, in my view, make with their readers. A sense of obligation leads to caring, and caring leads to commitment. To me, it's not pandering to seek to write stories that meet my readers' needs and desires—it's respect. When you honor your readers by understanding them, they'll honor you by becoming loyal fans.

UNDERSTAND YOUR READERS' EXPECTATIONS

If you want to satisfy your readers, you need to know what they look for in the books they read. Every genre has conventions, and understanding those conventions allows you to honor them as well as your readers. Consider these common fiction genres:

- **LITERARY FICTION:** character driven; usually about a transitional passage in life, such as coming-of-age, overcoming abandonment, facing mortality, and the like; or reflects on global themes, such as good vs. evil or autonomy vs. interdependency.
- **POPULAR FICTION** (also known as commercial or genre fiction): plot driven; subgenres include crime fiction, fantasy, romance, horror, and science fiction/speculative (often called sci fi and spec)

The term *narrative nonfiction* (sometimes called *creative nonfiction* or *literary nonfiction*) refers to a broad range of work that meets the definition included in *Creative Nonfiction*'s banner, "True stories, well told." Narrative nonfiction handles reality using the same techniques novelists use to create relatability, understanding, and immediacy—among them, suspense. Using the craft techniques commonly associated with fiction, such as dialogue and description, narrative nonfiction focuses on telling the emotional truth underlying factual incidents. The two most common forms of narrative nonfiction are:

- **MEMOIR:** a personal story. While an autobiography follows a chronological structure, a memoir shares a themed slice of life. Subgenres run a wide gamut from travelogues to overcoming obstacles such as drug addition, mental illness, or surviving a wrenching loss. A memoir tells the author's story.
- **LITERARY JOURNALISM** (also called *narrative journalism*): a public story. Subgenres include celebrity profiles, industry profiles of fields, such as baseball or beer-making, and true crime, among many others. In literary journalism, the author tells someone else's story.

Your writing goal is to put a fresh spin on a familiar story. You don't want to be imitative or formulaic, but you do want to adhere to the single most significant principle of writing success—write about relatable characters' longings.

ANALYZE GENRE CONVENTIONS

To know your reader expectations, you must know your genre. Crime fiction, for instance, which is itself a subgenre of popular fiction, features a dozen or more sub-subgenres, each of which comes with its own set of conventions. For example, here are some of the sub-subgenres that fall under the umbrella term crime fiction:

- Traditional
- Paranormal
- Historical

- Romantic suspense
- Police procedural
- Private eye
- Hard-boiled
- Soft-boiled
- Women in jeopardy
- Noir
- Espionage
- Thrillers

There are often subgenres of sub-subgenres, too. For instance, in thrillers, you'll find legal thrillers, medical thrillers, political thrillers, and the like. In traditional mysteries, you'll find cozies and craft- or animal-themed stories, among others.

I write cozies, a subgenre of traditional mysteries, which is a subgenre under the crime fiction umbrella and which is profoundly different from another popular subgenre—thrillers. While traditional mysteries and thrillers share attributes (they both feature a crime, for instance), they are on opposite ends of the crime fiction spectrum. A traditional mystery is a whodunit, whereas a thriller is a how-can-we-stop-them-from-doing-it. As you compare these seemingly opposite subgenres in Figure 1.1, you'll note that although they differ in essential ways, they share a fundamental element—the use of suspense.

FIGURE 1.1: KNOW YOUR GENRE

GENRE: Traditional mystery

VICTIM/KILLER RELATIONSHIP: Victim and killer are known to one another—no random serial killers.

MOTIVE: The motive is personal. Usually the motive is domestic in nature, fueled by love, hate, revenge, greed, or envy.

SEXUAL CONTENT: No explicit sex, although tasteful hugging and kissing are acceptable.

ONSTAGE VIOLENCE: No graphic violence; usually no onstage violence

USE OF OFFENSIVE LANGUAGE: No cussin'

ROLE OF FORENSICS: The solution depends on the deductive ability of the sleuth; no or few forensics come into play. Some simple elements of science, such as fingerprint analyses, may be used in small doses.

SLEUTH CHARACTERISTICS: The protagonist is honorable and kind—and most of all, he is relatable.

KILLER CHARACTERISTICS: The murderer is often likeable, often a good person pushed to the edge—and most of all, he is relatable.

CONSEQUENCES OF SLEUTH FAILING: If the protagonist fails, the effect is personal. An unsolved murder, while disturbing and even frightening, doesn't threaten life as we know it.

SETTING: Usually a small town, and only in one place

PACE: Leisurely to steady

SUB-SUBGENRES: A sub-subgenre called a *cozy* often features an amateur sleuth. Other sub-subgenres incorporate animals involved in solving the crimes or a theme such as quilting, cooking, genealogy, gardening, antiquing, etc.

GENRE: Thriller

VICTIM/KILLER RELATIONSHIP: The victims and killer are often strangers; the victims are often pawns in the killer's machinations.

MOTIVE: The motive is impersonal, although it may have its origins in a personal issue, for instance, a man who's fired and decides to kill all the company's employees. Sometimes the killer is mentally ill. Sometimes he has a motive that, in the spy business, is known as "MICE," an acronym coined to describe why people become traitors to their nations (money, ideology, conspiracy, ego).

SEXUAL CONTENT: Much sexual content or implication, often explicit

ONSTAGE VIOLENCE: Graphic, onstage violence

USE OF OFFENSIVE LANGUAGE: Liberal use of swearing and offensive language

ROLE OF FORENSICS: Often, forensics and high-tech gadgets figure prominently in the solution.

SLEUTH CHARACTERISTICS: The protagonist is a really, really noble good guy—a worthy hero.

KILLER CHARACTERISTICS: The murderer is a really, really evil bad guy—a worthy villain.

CONSEQUENCES OF SLEUTH FAILING: The consequences of the hero's failure to stop the bad guy are of global proportions—literally, such as the end of the world, or figuratively, such as the death of a child.

SETTING: One or more locations, ranging from isolated, off-the-grid places to big cities, often with a global sweep

PACE: Fast, against a ticking clock

SUB-SUBGENRES: Many sub-subgenres featuring specializations such as politics, medicine, espionage, legal, technology, etc.

IDENTIFY READER EXPECTATIONS

To begin to understand your readers, look to their favorite books. Select six or more beloved and/or best-selling examples from within your chosen genre. As you read or reread them, track key elements such as those pinpointed in Figure 1.1. You can adapt that model for whatever genre you're working in.

THE NARRATIVE QUESTION

The narrative question refers to the overarching thematic question posed at the beginning of the book that must be answered by the end. As such, your narrative questions form a kind of contract with the reader. Narrative questions are rarely posed in the form of actual questions; rather, they're implicit in the situation you create.

The sooner you introduce the narrative question, the better. Don't think your readers will patiently follow along as you set the scene. You need to hook their interest right away. (Part of this determination depends on pacing, which is discussed in chapter three.)

You've no doubt heard of Chekhov's gun; the principle that everything mentioned in your story must serve a purpose. Chekhov wrote, "Remove everything that has no relevance to the story. If you say in the first chapter that there is a rifle hanging on the wall, in the second or third chapter it absolutely must go off. If it's not going to be fired, it shouldn't be hanging there." The narrative question follows a similar principle. Don't pose a question at the start of your book if you don't intend to answer it; likewise, any questions raised must be fundamental to the story.

Figure 1.2 shows how the narrative question and other key factors come into play in historical romance. For this analysis, I chose two enduringly popular novels written by best-selling author Georgette Heyer.

Heyer wrote more than fifty novels, most of them historical romances. *Frederica*, set during the English Regency (1811 to 1820), tells the story of a twenty-four-year-old woman who is left in charge of her younger siblings after her parents die. Determined to launch her beautiful sister into London society, Frederica convinces the aloof Marquis of Alverstoke to help. In *Black Sheep*, another of her Regency romances, we meet Abigail and Miles. Twenty-eight-year-old Abby has an overdeveloped sense of familial duty; forty-year-old Miles has none.

FIGURE 1.2: ANALYZE KEY FACTORS

TITLE: *Frederica*

PROTAGONIST MOTIVATION: Frederica: to introduce her beautiful younger sister, Charis, into London society

ANTAGONIST MOTIVATION: The Marquis of Alverstoke: to annoy his demanding sister Louisa and his equally demanding cousin, Lucretia

NARRATIVE QUESTION: Will Frederica, who doesn't spare a thought for her own future, find happiness?

THEME: Love conquers all.

SEXUAL CONTENT: Romantic longing is shown, but no explicit sex. For instance, when Charis makes doe eyes at a man, you feel her passion. There are occasional touches and cuddles.

SETTING: London and its environs during the Regency

PACE: Leisurely

MASTERING SUSPENSE, STRUCTURE, & PLOT

STRUCTURE: Chronological, over the course of a few months

SUSPENSE: Overall, will Frederica and Alverstoke's goals be met? Specifically, will Charis get her way? Will Frederica's youngest brother be killed? Will her oldest brother sabotage her plans?

TITLE: *Black Sheep*

PROTAGONIST MOTIVATION: Abigail: to keep her beloved niece, Fanny, from throwing herself away on a fortune hunter

ANTAGONIST MOTIVATION: Miles: to marry Abby

NARRATIVE QUESTION: Will Abby succumb to the pressure of her family?

THEME: Adults make independent decisions.

SEXUAL CONTENT: Romantic longing is shown, but no explicit sex. For example, Miles's eyes glint when he looks at Abby, and her pulse races when she meets his passionate gaze.

SETTING: Bath, England

PACE: Leisurely

STRUCTURE: Chronological, over the course of a few months

SUSPENSE: Overall, will Abby and Miles's goals be met? Specifically, will the mysterious Mrs. Clapham succeed in detaching Fanny from her ne'er-do-well lover?

FIGURE 1.3: ANALYZE THE BEST OF YOUR GENRE

Now it's your turn to put this analytical approach to work for your own story. Apply the list below to six books in your genre. The list of factors is intended to be a guide, not a straightjacket. Feel free to tweak it to include factors that pertain to your genre. Remember to always include structure (discussed in chapter two) and to track suspense, as these crucial factors cross genre lines.

- Protagonist Motivation:
- Antagonist Motivation:
- Narrative Question:
- Theme:
- Sexual Content:

- Setting:
- Pace:
- Structure:
- Suspense:
- What Else?

Having analyzed key elements of favorite or best-selling examples within your genre to acquire a comprehensive understanding of your readers' expectations, you're ready to begin developing your story. The next step is selecting the framework for that story—its structure.

CHAPTER TWO

STRUCTURE IS KING

 The higher your structure is to be, the deeper must be its foundation.
—SAINT AUGUSTINE

FRAME YOUR PLOT WITH STRUCTURE

Structure is an organizing principle that once set will help you develop and write your stories. Structures can be linear or non-linear, simple or complex, drifting or charging in and out of time and place, featuring any number of perspectives and points of view. Different stories lend themselves to different structures, and there is no right or wrong decision. The only mistake you can make is having no structure at all.

I know too well the downside of deciding structure doesn't matter. The first novel I wrote, *Exposed*, suffered from a lack of architecture. *Exposed* was a mystery featuring a private eye named Tony Barnes. I loved Tony. I still do. I relished telling Tony's story—all of it—not only what pertained to the mystery, but a fair amount about his family, too. Instead of a tightly woven plot, I'd created a rambling narrative about a fictional character. There was no structure, just a muddled heap of words on the page. It's no surprise the book didn't sell. Choose a compelling structure, and your stories will enjoy a happier fate.

CHOOSE FROM TWO RELIABLE OPTIONS

From Aristotle's admonition that stories needed a beginning, a middle, and an end to nineteenth-century novelist Gustav Freytag's storytelling analysis (commonly known as Freytag's pyramid or Freytag's triangle), the idea of selecting an organizing principle is not new. In this chapter, I'll aim to simplify the process so you can easily choose a structure that's right for your work.

The two major structural approaches are linear (also called chronological) and nonlinear. Both approaches can be combined with enhancements such as bookends, categories, or flashbacks (or flash-forwards). While these are by no means the only structural options, they're reliable, and they work predictably to support your story.

GLOSSARY

Understanding how these three factors differ from one another allows you to make sensible decisions about each one.

STRUCTURE: Your overall organizational framework

POINT OF VIEW: Your voice (i.e., first person, second person, third person, or omniscient)

PERSPECTIVE: Whose story is being told

Use Linear for Simplicity and Clarity

The chronological structure follows a regular, linear time line. Sometimes this chronological approach is inherent in the story line. For instance, in James Grady's 1974 thriller, *Six Days of the Condor*, the action takes place over the six days named in the title. (Interestingly, when the book was made into a movie, it became *Three Days of the Condor*.) Pulitzer Prize-winning author Carol Shields used the academic year to structure her 1976 novel *Small Ceremonies*. The novel's nine chapters run from September to May. Other times, chronology is the logical choice, the natural outcome of recounting consecutive events, as in Benjamin Franklin's autobiography, which starts with "Ancestors and Early Youth in Boston" and ends with "Agent of Pennsylvania in London," tracking his accomplishments from his birth in 1706 to his work in London (from 1757-1762 and 1764-1775.)

Use Nonlinear for Drama and Complexity

Your other option is to use a nonlinear structure, in which the time line is presented out of sequence. Nobel Prize-winner William Faulkner, long considered the master of the multiple perspective novel, created a complex example in his masterwork, *The Sound and the Fury*. This novel, which was selected by the Modern Library as one of the twentieth century's best books, includes four sections, each narrated by a different member of the Compson family. The novel shifts in time and place and perspective. In his *As I Lay Dying*, Faulkner takes this idea even further, telling the story through fifteen different characters who share fifty-nine chapters.

While nonlinear structures facilitate the telling of multiple story lines from varying points of view, they also can be overly complicated and sometimes even confusing. Before selecting a nonlinear structure, you should confirm its value for your particular project. For instance, if you're writing a family saga featuring Rebecca, a matriarch known for her quilting, you might organize the book by quilting patterns: Perhaps Rebecca created a quilt using the pattern called *Rocky Road to Kansas* during the time the family struggled to reach the frontier; she worked on a quilt called *Seaside Stiches* in the chapters that recount a pivotal summer experience; and she started a quilt known as *Amish Shadow* when one of her sons shocked the family by marrying an Amish girl; and so on. At the end, the quilts will figure into the resolution of all the individual story lines. Perhaps four generations of the family come together in the present day to honor Rebecca, who's just died. Each branch of the family brings one of her quilts. They take turns telling their stories, using their quilt as a jumping off point. At the end, they donate the collection to a local historical society, where it will be preserved and appreciated for generations. In this case, this nonlinear structure is a logical choice; it's harmonious with the underlying themes of family, warmth, self-reliance, and hard work.

Don't select a nonlinear structure to be different or fancy or because it intrigues you. Instead, select a structure that aligns with your story.

CHOOSE MULTIPLE PERSPECTIVES OR A SINGLE POV

Mysteries often use the multiple perspective structure, allowing both the hero and the villain their say, and sometimes, the victims, too. In Robert B. Parker's *Night Passage*, for example, each chapter is told from one character's point of view, although there are occasional shifts in perspective within chapters. Here's an analysis of the perspectives Parker used in the first fifth of the book:

- Chapter one: Jesse Stone, the protagonist
- Chapter two: Tom Carson, a victim

- Chapter three: Jesse Stone, the protagonist
- Chapter four: Hasty Hathaway, the antagonist
- Chapter five: Jesse Stone, the protagonist
- Chapter six: Jo-Jo Genest, the villain
- Chapter seven: Jesse Stone, the protagonist
- Chapter eight: Carole Genest, a victim; halfway through this chapter, the perspective changes to Jo-Jo, her ex-husband, for three sentences. (Note: Jo-Jo interjects his voice into his ex-wife's chapter, a perfect metaphor, given Jo-Jo's behavior—a subplot tracks Jo-Jo's efforts to interject himself into his ex-wife's life.)
- Chapter nine: Jesse Stone, the protagonist
- Chapter ten: Jo-Jo Genest, the villain
- Chapter eleven: Jesse Stone, the protagonist
- Chapter twelve: Hasty Hathaway, the antagonist
- Chapter thirteen: Jesse Stone, the protagonist
- Chapter fourteen: Jesse Stone, the protagonist
- Chapter fifteen: Jesse Stone, the protagonist (Note: The perspective shifts to Abby Taylor, Jesse's love interest, for two sentences, one in the middle of the chapter, the other near the end.)
- Chapter sixteen: Tom Carson, a victim
- Chapter seventeen: Abby Taylor, Jesse's love interest
- Chapter eighteen: Charlie Buck, a detective from Wyoming

Night Passage continues to follow this pattern, changing perspective chapter by chapter, with minor characters having their voices dominate fewer chapters than major characters, and no character presented more than Jesse. You'll note that despite the multiple perspectives, the story still follows a chronological structure. This technique allows the reader to observe how various characters think, to witness cause and effect, and to feel the rippling tension of growing suspense as deadly events are set in motion.

Changing points of view is tempting since it provides readers with a multifaceted perspective and allows you to delve deeply into different characters' lives and attitudes. Before you jump in, though, consider some of the ways this tactic can go wrong.

- Readers might lose interest in your story if they discover who the villain is before the protagonist figures it out.
- It's easy to reveal too much, too quickly, and doing so effectively negates suspense.
- Frequent switches in perspective can interrupt the narrative flow.

In addition, not all authors are able to write all kinds of characters believably. Some men have trouble writing from a female perspective, just as some women have trouble writing from a male perspective, for example. Some authors struggle with writing characters of certain ages (like children or the elderly), different cultures, or unfamiliar educational backgrounds.

I ran into this problem myself. I learned that it's one thing to write a scene that includes a child viewed from an adult's perspective, but it's another thing altogether to write the child from her own perspective. I worked for two years trying to get a twelve-year-old girl's voice to sound authentic. The girl was the protagonist in a short story called "Last Supper." The story, which ultimately was published in *Alfred Hitchcock Mystery Magazine*, follows a recently orphaned girl as she navigates her new world and finds herself mixed up in a murder. Consider how profoundly different the first lines of the final draft are compared to the first lines of the initial draft.

> **First draft:** The yellow police tape circling the old maples came into view. For three days now, walking from the school bus to the Morrisons' house, my house now, I'd hurried past the crime scene, but

today, even though my throat closed as if I'd swallowed a too-big piece of food, I stopped to look.

Final draft: I pinched myself real hard the way my used-to-be best friend, Jackie, taught me, and it worked, just like always—I stopped crying.

Doesn't the final draft sound more authentic? I figured it out, but writing from a preteen's perspective felt so unnatural to me, and took so much effort, I decided not to do it ever again. If I want to include a child or teenager in my story, that character is written from an adult's point of view and perspective.

Another way to gain the advantage of multiple points of view is to use the third-person omniscient voice, which allows shifts in perspective. Jane Austen employed this all-knowing voice in *Pride and Prejudice*, for example. While most of the narration is from Elizabeth's perspective, periodically information is shared that Elizabeth doesn't know, such as Charlotte's pursuit of Mr. Collins.

In her 1961 nonlinear novel, *The Prime of Miss Jean Brodie* (selected by *Time* magazine and Modern Library as a best novel), author Muriel Spark used a flash-forward to create a suspenseful and complex structure. The story, set in pre-World War II Scotland, follows the relationship between an unconventional teacher and six female students over an eight-year period. Early in the story we learn through a flash-forward, told by an omniscient narrator, that one of the six girls betrays Miss Brodie, but we aren't told which one. As we read about Miss Brodie's relationship with each of the girls, we wonder—is she the one who turned against her? Spark's use of an omniscient narrator works well, allowing the reader to see into the future.

The omniscient voice comes with challenges, though. While it imbues the narrator with infinite, godlike knowledge, it also facilitates telling, not showing. When writing from a specific perspective, say, a suburban housewife, a reader learns of her husband's anger when he tells her to shut up and storms out of the house. This is an example of a writer using incident to reveal emotion—the nasty words and ferocious exit *show* what the man is feeling. Since an omniscient narrator can easily explain what the man is feeling, you risk robbing the reader of the chance to be there in the room, watching the couple's fight unfold. If you choose an omniscient narrator, be vigilant to avoid the telling-not-showing trap and capitalize on the opportunity to deepen your characterizations.

While an omniscient narrator is a tempting choice because of its versatility and flexibility, often a single point of view is the best way to go. In traditional mysteries, for example, readers expect to experience everything your sleuth does as it happens, and you can achieve that only by maintaining a single point of view. Further, a single point of view is the most intimate of all the options. Your readers get to know your narrator well, and familiarity breeds friendship. I use the first-person singular point of view in my Josie stories, for instance. You see what Josie sees, as she sees it. You also are in the room observing how she feels about people and situations, and how she acts.

As with most writing decisions, while you may have dozens or even scores of options, the best choice is usually the one that is most in sync with your readers' expectations.

ADD ENHANCEMENTS TO INCREASE TENSION

Both linear and nonlinear structures can be enhanced by integrating other structural elements, such as bookends, categories, and flashbacks (or flash-forwards). These enhancements tighten the structure; the tighter the structure, the more your readers can focus on your plot, prose, and themes without having to wonder where they are in the story.

Bookends

Bookends provide an appealing thematic symmetry. With the bookend structure, you begin and end your story with the same motif. At the beginning, you set the stage; at the end, you complete the circle and return to that same stage. You give your readers the pleasure of thinking on a deeper level, of reflecting on bigger issues.

In my Josie Prescott Antiques Mysteries, for example, I bookend a chronological telling of the mystery with scenes of sweet interactions. I'll start with Josie at work or with a friend, drawing you into her world. I always end with a private, tender moment between Josie and her boyfriend, Ty. Readers of my kind of mysteries—cozies—want happy endings. The beginning of the book signals they're entering a safe and wholesome world. After the mystery is solved and chaos resolves into order, the world is once again safe and wholesome. This technique works no matter what mood you seek to create.

New York Times best-selling author J.T. Ellison wanted an ominous feel in her debut novel, the 2007 thriller *All the Pretty Girls*. The novel, about a sadistic serial killer, begins with a victim saying, "No," and ends with the detective who solves the crime saying, "Yes." Isn't that symmetry satisfying?

Bookends can also be used for nonlinear nonfiction. For instance, Elizabeth Gilbert's essay "The Muse of the Coyote Ugly Saloon," both begins and ends with a reference to who is the prettiest girl in the bar. The opening reference finds the narrator comparing herself to the other female bartenders—she isn't the prettiest girl in the bar. The closing reference has that same narrator recalling how, when she was a little girl, she would accompany her grandfather into bars. All the men fawned on her. She was always the prettiest girl in the bar. This duality shows how perceptions are formed and how they lead to choices some people might find peculiar.

In this essay, Gilbert recounts the narrator's experiences bartending in a dive, but we don't know why she's there until the end of the essay, when she explains her attraction to bars and the men who haunt them. At the beginning we wonder why a woman would take a job in a bar where she goes home every night drenched in beer and who knows what else. Once we learn that the narrator associates bars with male appreciation, her motivations become clear. The bookend structure contributes to a thematic understanding of the role of affirmation in a character's development.

The bookend structure serves to anchor your theme or themes. It enables the reader to slip into your world seamlessly, to get to know characters quickly, and to begin to reflect on your broad themes right from the start.

Categories

Categorizing content aids understanding and enriches readers' experiences. Categories can include places, people, activities, events, or anything else that helps clarify your themes.

In Elizabeth Gilbert's book-length memoir, *Eat, Pray, Love: One Woman's Search for Everything Across Italy, India and Indonesia*, she combines chronology with categories. As soon as you read the title you know the structure: You're going to read about the author's search across three continents, categorized as eating in Italy, praying in India, and finding love in Indonesia.

Italo Calvino's 1973 nonlinear novel, *The Castle of Crossed Destinies*, relied on tarot cards for its structure. Calvino laid out the cards in a grid, then, based on his reading of them from top to bottom and side to side, he wrote interconnected stories.

The novel is divided into two parts—"The Castle of Crossed Destinies" and "The Tavern of Crossed Destinies"—and follows two groups of travelers through a forest. All the travelers have lost their ability to speak. One group stays the night in a castle; the other stays in a tavern. In both locations, the travelers use tarot cards instead of words to share their stories, "talking" about their loves, their losses, and their adventures. A narrator interprets the tarot cards for the reader, but since tarot cards are open to manifold interpretations, the narrators often get the stories wrong. Moving through time and space, the use of tarot cards as a structural device highlights the book's themes of ambiguity and clarity in communications.

Keep in mind there is no one best category. Experiment with various alternatives. See which one best highlights your themes.

Flashbacks and Flash-Forwards

Using flashbacks and flash-forwards allows you to control the flow of information. You can have a character reveal backstory not by telling the story, but by showing the events. They also allow you to tell multiple stories emanating from different time periods.

Rex Stout wrote his Nero Wolfe detective stories using short-term flashbacks within a chronological telling of the story. Chapters typically begin with the first-person narrator, the assistant detective Archie Goodwin, setting the scene, referencing the day and time. Archie might say that it's Friday at noon, adding a general assessment of the current case they're investigating. After stating that not much had happened during the three days they've had the case, Archie segues into recounting the highlights of their efforts, then segues back to the present time. This shift in time feels natural because Archie seems to be chatting.

Junot Diaz's Pulitzer Prize-winning immigrant novel *The Brief Wondrous Life of Oscar Wao* uses flashbacks (and shifting perspectives and points of view) to tell two interwoven stories. One story line follows an obese Dominican-born boy, Oscar De Leòn, as he tries and fails to meet familial and cultural obligations; the other focuses on a curse that has haunted his family for as long as anyone can remember. Thematically, the novel considers what happens when an immigrant's cultural identity becomes diluted. The seemingly omniscient narrator is only revealed to be Oscar's college roommate, Yunior de Las Casas, toward the end of the book. Diaz's complex amalgam of chronology, with flashbacks and shifting perspectives, demonstrates the elasticity of structure.

Flashbacks can backfire, though. If they're no more than thinly veiled excuses for an info-dump, usually over-explaining backstory or providing too-long stretches of exposition, readers lose interest in the story. Even if the content of a flashback is meaningful and well written, it can still be distracting; there you are, into the story, and boom—your concentration is broken. The best way to integrate flashbacks is to connect the ending of the scene happening in the current time frame with the beginning of the flashback.

In Case Study #1, for example, I could write: "A long-forgotten sense of paralyzing dread turned Kayla's blood to ice. She hadn't heard that particular click-snap since she was ten, the day Morris, a boy she thought was her friend, shot up her school. It was the sound of an automatic pistol being reloaded." The next chapter could open with Kayla huddled in a corner of her fifth-grade classroom, the teacher whispering that everything would be all right, that everything was fine, be quiet now, shhhh. When handled smoothly, flashbacks can heighten readers' interest in your characters. Since readers get to know the characters at different periods of their lives, they can relate to them on a deeper level.

Flash-forwards can intensify suspense by creating a sense of impending doom. We, the readers, know that disaster looms for Miss Brodie in *The Prime of Miss Jean Brodie* (discussed earlier in this chapter), but she does not. Flash-forwards can also serve to illuminate characters' behavior. For example, Charles Dickens used a flash-forward in his 1843 novella, *A Christmas Carol*, to explain Scrooge's transformation from parsimonious and mean-spirited to generous and kind. Scrooge is visited by the Ghost of Christmas Yet to Come, who shows him scenes surrounding the death of a "wretched man." When Scrooge learns that this unloved soul is his own he's shocked and alarmed. He weeps over his own neglected grave. He awakens, back in the present, repentant, a changed man.

You need to be careful not to overuse the technique, though, since flash-forwards break the narrative flow and can feel heavy-handed if not used in small doses and for a specific purpose.

You can do whatever you choose, of course, regarding structure, point of view, and perspective, as long as you align it with your theme and the other factors we've discussed. Don't ever feel you're on a hunt for the one structure that will work. There are countless effective approaches. Select the one or ones that strike a chord in you, and write with confidence, knowing you can always change your mind.

CHOOSE YOUR STRUCTURE

Since there's no one structure that works in all situations, you need to make a decision based on the key elements of your story, your theme or unifying principle, and your preference. Figure 2.1, which uses the two case studies described in the introduction as examples, shows you one way to select a structure. Case Study #1, you'll recall, is a domestic thriller; Case Study #2 is a memoir. As you read through Figure 2.1, note how the questions help you think through your decision about structure.

FIGURE 2.1: THINK FIRST, THEN WRITE

CASE STUDY #1: DOMESTIC THRILLER
Whose story is it? Kayla, a recently divorced office manager and noncustodial mother of two
What's your theme? Be careful whom you trust.
Over what time span does the story occur? Three days.
What's the narrative question? Will Kayla be able to save herself from the diabolical plot against her?
Structure options: Linear or nonlinear, single or shifting perspective, with or without bookends, categories, and flashbacks (or flash-forwards)

CASE STUDY #2: MEMOIR
Whose story is it? Al, a junior high school math teacher
What's your theme? If you don't help yourself first, you can't help anyone else.
Over what time span does the story occur? A year.
What's the narrative question? Will Al be able to continue meeting the needs of the people he loves: his wife, Mary, a banker; his dad, Hamilton, a retired lawyer; his sister, Kathy, a software company executive; and his rebellious teenage son, Stewart?
Structure options: Linear or nonlinear, single or shifting perspective, with or without bookends, categories, and flashbacks (or flash-forwards)

Think about the implications of each decision. If you use chronology in your thriller, you're likely to decide to start in the middle of the inciting incident—in this example, the moment Kayla realizes her purse is gone. If you want bookends, too, you'll want to think about something meaningful to Kayla that relates to trust, your theme. Start thinking of ways to juxtapose trust and betrayal. Perhaps someone she trusted lets her down at the start, while someone she doesn't trust surprises her with kindness at the end.

If you decide to go with shifting perspectives, you could have the villain start the narrative, perhaps planning his attack, then switch to Kayla in the grocery store. Or you could start with Kayla in the grocery store, then switch to the villain, perhaps one of the people in the crowd, watching as she rushes into the parking lot hoping to see the thief running away, her purse wedged under his arm like a football. Your plot, even at this early stage, is coming together.

FAQ

Q: I'm writing a young adult fantasy. What structure should I use?

A: You can use any of the structures discussed in this chapter. Before choosing, though, you should complete the exercise in chapter one and the one that follows (See Figure 2.2). These two exercises will help ensure you've considered all the factors that might impact your decision. For instance, is your novel essentially a thriller that occurs in a phantasmal world? Is it a romance? A literary novel? Let your knowledge of your readers and the core elements of your story guide your decision.

The same structural choices are presented for the second case study, a memoir. Almost by definition, most memoirs are told from a single perspective using a linear chronological structure. It's natural. It fits. Yet it's worth considering whether other options might work, too. As you can see from my analysis in Figure 2.1, the pressure Al is feeling comes from his efforts to satisfy other people's needs. It isn't only Al's story. Who says you can't use a shifting perspective structure in a memoir? You could have Al imagine what other people are thinking and feeling, or perhaps he could ask them for their perceptions of various situations, then translate their comments into chapters from their perspectives.

FIGURE 2.2: CONSIDER YOUR STRUCTURE

As you complete the Consider Your Structure questions, it's important to remember that once you begin plotting in earnest, if you find the structure you selected isn't working, you can always change it. The questions are intended to help guide your thinking, not to lock you in to any one choice.

- Whose story is it?
- What's your theme?
- Over what time span does the story occur?
- What's your narrative question?
- Structure options:

Structure truly is king. It organizes and frames your story, allowing you to write efficiently and with confidence. With your readers' expectations clear in your mind and a structure selected, you're ready to plot.

CHAPTER THREE

JANE'S PLOTTING ROAD MAP

> 66 What is character but the determination of incident? What is incident but the illustration of character? 99
>
> —HENRY JAMES

I write from a detailed synopsis, and I encourage you to do the same—or at least to give it a try. To some people, adopting this kind of methodical approach is the antithesis of innovation. To me, it fosters creativity and helps traverse the landscape of conflicting and confusing choices like a sextant guides a sailor across the sea. Without an organizational scaffold, ideas are likely to slip away while confusion snowballs. My synopsis is a formal written document, but whether you outline, organize your plot points on index cards, or are one of the few able to keep it all in your head, to write efficiently, you need first to codify your story.

The one time I didn't write from a synopsis, I had to rewrite the entire manuscript. Not merely revise it—I had to reimagine it and to redo it from start to finish. I'd gone off on tangents that interested me but didn't move the story forward, got bogged down in irrelevant details, and lost track of plot points. The manuscript was a mess. I'll never forget how my stomach plummeted as I listened to my St. Martin's Minotaur editor describe the problems. (This is the same editor, by the way, who helped me understand that I was writing cozies.) In this case, she was so concerned that I wouldn't be able to salvage the novel—that no one could—she took me to lunch to break the news gently. I promised her I would fix it quickly, and I did. I had to. If I'd bollixed up their production cycle, a bad situation would have been made infinitely worse.

FAQ

Q: How do you know if the feedback you get is on the mark? Everyone is entitled to his or her opinion, but that doesn't make it right.

A: In the prepublication stages of writing, separating the wheat from the chaff of feedback is one of your toughest jobs as an author. Just because you might receive some feedback that wasn't helpful, though, doesn't mean you should dismiss the process out of hand by discounting the value of constructive criticism. As Bill Gates said, "We all need people who will give us feedback. It's how we improve." One trick that may work for you is to move beyond *what* the person thinks needs changing and ask *why*. This one question helps differentiate thoughtful, considered opinions from gut reactions. (Not that gut reactions are intrinsically suspect, but they're often based solely on one person's emotional response, which may or may not reflect your broader audience's reactions.) Once you're working with an agent and professional editors, however, the dynamic shifts. These folks know what readers want, and their only goal is to help your work succeed in the marketplace. I routinely do as my agent and editors recommend, and my work always gets better.

When the book was finally accepted for publication, I sat down for a good heart-to-heart talk with myself. I needed to analyze how I'd gotten so far off track. I had enjoyed writing the book. I'd been fascinated by the direction my characters had taken me. I was confident in my prose. What, I asked myself, went wrong? It didn't take me long to realize the big issue—it is diabolically easy for me to get lost in my stories, following whatever track interests me at that moment with no thought of the bigger picture, the plot. To avoid finding myself adrift yet again, I needed a map.

My goal was to mitigate risk and increase efficiency. I didn't want to rely on serendipity; I wanted to rely on myself. It seems to me you're born with talent, or not; that opportunities knock, or they don't; and the only prong on this triad of success in your control is self-discipline. I needed a system I could rely on. It took me a year of false starts and refinement, but since creating Jane's Plotting Road Map, I've written eight more novels and three short stories, all published by St. Martin's Minotaur and *Alfred Hitchcock Mystery Magazine*. This proves, it would appear, that my system works. Using Jane's Plotting Road Map (Figure 3.1) will help you circumnavigate your writing world, too.

FIGURE 3.1: JANE'S PLOTTING ROAD MAP

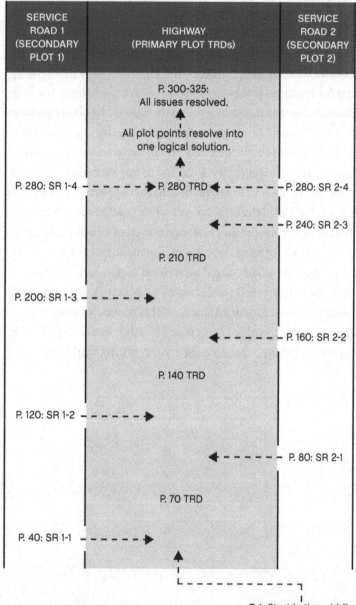

SERVICE ROAD 1 (SECONDARY PLOT 1)	HIGHWAY (PRIMARY PLOT TRDs)	SERVICE ROAD 2 (SECONDARY PLOT 2)
	P. 300-325: All issues resolved.	
	All plot points resolve into one logical solution.	
P. 280: SR 1-4	P. 280 TRD	P. 280: SR 2-4
		P. 240: SR 2-3
	P. 210 TRD	
P. 200: SR 1-3		
		P. 160: SR 2-2
	P. 140 TRD	
P. 120: SR 1-2		
		P. 80: SR 2-1
	P. 70 TRD	
P. 40: SR 1-1		

P. 1: Start in the middle of the inciting incident.

MASTERING SUSPENSE, STRUCTURE, & PLOT

The major elements of Jane's Plotting Road Map include the highway, service roads, and TRDs (twists/reversals/dangers). The highway, which runs from the bottom to the top, represents the path your primary plot will follow. Service Road #1 and Service Road #2, abbreviated as SR#1 and SR#2, are located on either side of the highway and represent the paths of your two subplots (discussed in chapter five).

TRDs include plot twists, plot reversals, or moments of heightened danger, and are a key to effective storytelling. In most books of about 300 to 325 pages (formatted for submission—Times New Roman, 12 point, double-spaced, normal margins, not justified right, and no extra space between paragraphs), you should plan for four TRDs that occur every 70 to 90 pages. In Figure 3.1, they are placed along the main highway at pages 70, 140, 210, and 280. In addition to TRDs, you should insert a scene relating to one of your subplots (alternating between them) approximately every 40 pages. Follow this pattern to the end, and all three plotlines will weave together in a seamless, satisfactory conclusion.

Using Jane's Plotting Road Map guarantees your story will be multilayered but not confusing. Most readers won't be aware of the structural rhythm you've created; they'll simply perceive that your story is impossible to put down, appropriately paced, and wonderfully intricate.

FIND FRESH IDEAS

Jane's Plotting Road Map will help you develop a compelling plot whether you know every detail of your story from start to finish or barely have a glimmer of an idea. When I start plotting a Josie mystery, I think about my story's beginning and end. In addition, I never lose sight of my broad theme, my protagonist, and the other factors that lead to a complex plot. Figure 3.2 shows how these elements come into play in a variety of genres, including a historical romance, a literary novel, a middle school mystery, a memoir, one of my "Josie" novels, and our two case studies.

FIGURE 3.2

TITLE/AUTHOR: *Frederica* by Georgette Heyer

GENRE: Historical romance

PROTAGONIST: Frederica, the twenty-four-year-old head of her household, is determined to launch her beautiful younger sister, Charis, into London society.

BEGINNING: The Marquis of Alverstoke refuses to host a grand ball to launch his niece into London society.

NARRATIVE QUESTION(S): Will Frederica, who doesn't spare a thought for her own future, find happiness?

END: Frederica acknowledges that the life she dreamed of for her sister, Charis, is not the life Charis dreamed of for herself. Frederica accepts the Marquis of Alverstoke's marriage proposal.

BROAD THEMES: You're more likely to find love when you aren't looking for it.

OVERARCHING STRUCTURE: Chronological

PACE: Leisurely

TITLE/AUTHOR: *Nightwork* by Irwin Shaw

GENRE: Literary fiction

PROTAGONIST: Douglas Grimes, an ex-pilot who's down on his luck, steals what is to him a fortune, thus gambling on his future.

BEGINNING: An unnamed man working the graveyard shift at the front desk at a seedy New York City hotel selects his bet on tomorrow's horse race. He has no hope for his future. His bad eyes cost him his pilot's job, and he's a gambler.

NARRATIVE QUESTION(S): Will the shy, self-effacing protagonist find happiness after losing his dream?

END: The man completes his reinvention, and is ready to live the rest of his life in his new persona.

BROAD THEMES: You can reinvent yourself.

OVERARCHING STRUCTURE: Nonlinear chronological

PACE: Steady

TITLE/AUTHOR: *The London Eye Mystery* by Siobhan Dowd

GENRE: Middle school mystery

PROTAGONIST: Ted, who is somewhere on the autism spectrum (although that word is never used in the book), is determined to be a regular kid.

BEGINNING: Twelve-year-old Ted, whose brain works on a special operating system, and his fifteen-year-old sister, Kat, wait for their thirteen-year-old cousin, Salim, to come off London's huge Ferris wheel, the London Eye. He got on, but he doesn't get off.

NARRATIVE QUESTION(S): Will Salim be found? Will Ted be able to help with the investigation?

END: Ted, having solved the mystery, says goodbye to Salim as he and his mother head off to New York. Ted, eager to learn to communicate better, tells his sister a white lie, his first ever.

BROAD THEMES: Just because your brain works differently from other people's doesn't mean your way is wrong.

OVERARCHING STRUCTURE: Chronological

PACE: Steady

TITLE/AUTHOR: *Larry's Kidney* by Daniel Asa Rose

GENRE: Memoir

PROTAGONIST: Dan, a middle-aged writer, thought his adventures were behind him.

BEGINNING: The author's scapegrace and long-lost cousin, Larry, calls and asks the author to accompany him to China on a hunt for a desperately needed kidney replacement.

NARRATIVE QUESTION(S): Will Larry get his new kidney? Will the two men be arrested? Will Dan and Larry reconcile?

END: Just as Dan traveled alone to China, he travels home alone. Larry got his kidney, but remains as incorrigible as ever.

BROAD THEMES: Try to fight off death; take charge of your own health; family first.

OVERARCHING STRUCTURE: Chronological, with bookends

PACE: Leisurely

TITLE/AUTHOR: *Ornaments of Death*, a Josie Prescott Antiques Mystery by Jane K. Cleland

GENRE: Traditional (cozy) mystery

PROTAGONIST: Josie, an antiques appraiser and clever business woman, uses her knowledge of antiques to solve crimes.

BEGINNING: Two of Josie's employees, Gretchen and Eric, take her on a tour of her company's auction venue. They've transformed it into a winter wonderland for the company's annual holiday party.

NARRATIVE QUESTION(S): Will the killer be caught? Will Josie's new-found family live up to her expectations?

END: Josie and her boyfriend, Ty, sit in her cozy living room on Christmas Day, their love palpable.

BROAD THEMES: Order is restored from chaos; the killer is always punished.

OVERARCHING STRUCTURE: Chronological, with bookends

PACE: Steady

TITLE/AUTHOR: Case Study #1

GENRE: Domestic thriller

PROTAGONIST: Kayla, a recently divorced office manager and non-custodial mother of two, just wants peace.

BEGINNING: Kayla reaches for a box of cereal in her suburban grocery store. When she turns back to her cart, she discovers that her purse is gone.

NARRATIVE QUESTION(S): Will Kayla survive the mysterious attack against her? Will she be able to find her own strength?

END: Kayla closes her front door for the last time, ready to start her new life.

BROAD THEMES: Be careful whom you trust.

OVERARCHING STRUCTURE: Shifting POV

PACE: Fast

TITLE/AUTHOR: Case Study #2

GENRE: Memoir

PROTAGONIST: Al, a junior high school math teacher feels like he's up to his armpits in alligators. His wife, Mary, a banker, is impatient; his dad, Hamilton, a retired lawyer, is frustrated; his sister, Kathy, is nowhere to be seen; and his rebellious teenage son, Stewart, is out for blood

> **BEGINNING:** Al sits in his home office waiting for a reply to the text he just sent his sister. Their dad is refusing to get out of bed—again. The phone rings. It's the police. His teenage son, Stewart, has been arrested—again.
>
> **NARRATIVE QUESTION(S):** Will Al lose everything he values?
>
> **END:** Al sits in his home office, reads a text from his sister reporting that Dad is doing as well as can be expected, then turns off his smartphone and smiles.
>
> **BROAD THEMES:** If you don't help yourself first, you can't help anyone else.
>
> **OVERARCHING STRUCTURE:** Chronological, with bookends
>
> **PACE:** Steady

Don't fret if you don't have the kind of clarity reflected in Figure 3.2. It will come to you as you work with Jane's Plotting Road Map. Because you'll be traveling down the highway in units of time and distance, your story will develop logically. You don't have to plan the whole trip in advance; all you need to do is decide on the next TRD. There is an old Chinese saying that the longest journey begins with a single step. Jane's Plotting Road Map will help you embark on your journey by giving you the confidence of knowing you're on the right path.

SELECT YOUR TRDS

Let's define our terms.

- **TWISTS:** A plot twist takes the reader in an unexpected direction.
- **REVERSAL:** A reversal takes the story in the opposite direction to what the reader expects.
- **DANGER:** Moments of heightened danger can be physical (e.g., someone brandishes a knife) or emotional (e.g., you see in your lover's eyes that your heart is about to be broken).

As you evaluate which of the three options to choose at any point along the highway, remember to mix it up. Unless you're working in a very short form, you're going to have more than one TRD. For example, in the mini-memoir you read earlier about my mom getting into grad school, I created suspense by integrating a reversal. You thought I was going to be dealing with bad news, a family emergency; instead I got good news, my mom got into grad school. If I had stepped into my mom's living room and found a cousin who needed my help, then that would have been a twist—a surprising, sideways movement. If, when I got home, I found a thug holding a gun to my mom's head, then that would be a moment of heightened danger.

Note that by integrating TRDs as part of your prewriting planning process, you're certain to keep the story moving at the pace you think is best. Integrating one TRD at a time, you'll reach the end of your story with twisty delight.

DETERMINE THE APPROPRIATE PACE

Just as selecting a structure is crucial to storytelling success, so too is determining the rate of travel—your pace. Before you plot, choose the pace you plan on maintaining. Knowing the conventions of your chosen genre will help you decide which pace is suitable for your project. In general, pace can be categorized as leisurely, steady, or fast.

- **LEISURELY:** Adapt Jane's Plotting Road Map so TRDs occur every ninety to 110 pages.
- **STEADY:** You can use Jane's Plotting Road Map as drawn.
- **FAST:** Adapt Jane's Plotting Road Map so TRDs occur every thirty to fifty pages, or even more often.

Once you determine the proper speed, you can easily adjust the pace. You're in control of your readers' experience. If you want to take your readers on a more leisurely trip, reduce the frequency of TRDs; to speed up the pace, increase the frequency of TRDs. It's tempting to think a faster pace is always ideal, but it isn't. Since different genres come with different pacing imperatives, knowing what's suitable for your genre helps you make sensible decisions. Some genres move at quite a leisurely pace; others speed along with barely a moment's pause for breath. Most books, though, adopt a steady pace. Continue analyzing those books in your chosen genre that you admire, and model on their success.

One of my students, Justin O'Donnell, did just that. Justin is working on a novel called *The Last Saxon*. "It is the year 1066," Justin explained, "and the King of England is dead. A young Saxon finds himself thrust into a war that could change England forever, sending him on a journey of survival, vengeance, redemption, love, and salvation—for both himself and the land he calls home." Justin and I selected two books as exemplars for his project, Bernard Cornwell's *Agincourt* and Dan Brown's *The Da Vinci Code*. Justin's analysis of the two is detailed in Figure 3.3.

FIGURE 3.3: SAMPLE TRD ANALYSES

Vive le . . . English?

Bernard Cornwell's *Agincourt* kept my undivided attention for 430 pages. The tale follows a yeoman archer from England named Nicholas Hook. Twists, reversals, and moments of heightened danger occur at every turn. I have listed them in chronological order (annotated as "T" for twist; "R" for reversal; and "D" for heightened danger).

- P. 8 "D": Hook tries to settle a family feud by murdering a rival. He fails. His Lord finds out and sends him south to join the war.
- P. 27 "R": Hook saves a woman from being raped by a priest (Sir Martin). He punches the priest, which results in a death sentence for Hook. A sergeant helps Hook escape as an outlaw.
- P. 61 "D": Battle of Soissons begins (siege).

- P. 80 "R": Soissons sacked and betrayed from within. Hook saves a nun and kills his former commander, who was the traitor.
- P. 102 "R": Hook meets the King of England, Henry V. Henry pardons Hook of all crimes and commits him to service with Sir John—England's greatest warrior.
- P. 120 "D": Sir Martin and his group come across Hook and nearly kill him in London; Sir John interrupts the attack and saves Hook.
- P. 140 "T": Melisandre reveals to Hook who her father was (Lord Lanferelle—he was at Soissons watching English archers get tortured.) She admits that he raped her before he committed her to the nunnery as a way to repent of his sins. She was one of his bastard children.
- P. 168 "D": England invades France and lays siege to the city of Harfleur. Skirmishes.
- P. 174 "R": Lord Lanferelle catches Hook and some archers foraging; he kills some, then cuts off Hook's pinky finger and promises to kill him later in the war.
- P. 180 "T": Hook promoted to sergeant by Sir John.
- P. 201 "D": The English try to dig a mine under the besieged city's walls; the French dig a countermine and ambush the English.
- P. 203 "T": Perrill brothers (from the family feud) attempt to kill Hook during the chaos inside the mine.
- P. 209 "D": The mine collapses; Hook kills one of the Perrill brothers.
- P. 210 "D": The English camp is hit by dysentery.
- P. 218 "D": The French sally forth.
- P. 240 "D": The English counterattack and take part of the city; the French refuse to surrender. The English army is weak and depleted and cannot last much longer.
- P. 250 "R": French soldiers randomly surrender.
- P. 267 "T": Prisoner exchange. The English meet the French Marshal. The two countries share a humane, almost friendly exchange.
- P. 273 "R": Reinforcements arrive in Harfleur; Hook's brother is with them!
- P. 275 "R": The battered English army expects to return to England since the campaigning season is over, but King Henry changes his mind and marches them into the heart of France.

MASTERING SUSPENSE, STRUCTURE, & PLOT

- P. 283 "T": Hook and Melisandre marry in a church; the English learn the Burgundians have betrayed them by joining France.
- P. 295 "D": A messenger tells the English army the French army is massive and has been spotted. The French can attack them at any time.
- P. 300 "R": Henry stops the army because someone stole from a local priest. King Henry orders the culprit hanged; the culprit is Hook's brother, who was framed by Sir Martin and the Perrill brothers! Dead.
- P. 312 "D": The English stumble upon evidence of a trampled field, indicating the French army is very close. A game of cat and mouse ensues between the two armies.
- P. 314 "R": Just when the English are about to escape France, they stumble upon the entire French army blocking their path to the beach.
- P. 351 "D": On the cusp of battle, King Henry V gives his famous St. Crispin's Day speech.
- P. 358 "D": The Battle of Agincourt begins.
- P. 371 "D": Sir Martin corners Melisandre during the battle, planning to rape her.
- P. 376 "D": English archers run out of arrows vs. French army.
- P. 394: "D": The English men-at-arms blunt the French attack; the French turn to attack the unarmed archers.
- P. 396 "R": The French soldiers' steel boots get stuck in mud (slow); the English archers are nimble and begin to slaughter the heavily armed French.
- P. 401 "R": Just as she is about to be raped, Melisandre kills Sir Martin with a crossbow.
- P. 410 "D": Hook vs. Lord Lanferelle; Sir John interrupts their altercation, and the two great champions duel for their perspective countries.
- P. 416 "T": Hook saves Sir John before Lord Lanferelle can kill him.
- P. 423 "R": The English capture many French prisoners, but they don't have enough men left to guard them. King Henry orders all prisoners executed before the French attack again.
- P. 429 "T": Hook allows Lord Lanferelle to kill Tom Perrill and escape.
- P. 430 "R": English win against five-to-one odds.
- Epilogue: Tom and Melisandre return to England to start their lives together.

Pacing: This is obviously a modern book. It's no wonder most people consider Bernard Cornwell the best historical fiction author alive today. Something exciting happens every ten or twenty pages. I can't think of anything to cut. I went into this book not sure what to expect, but now I believe it to be one of the best historical novels I have ever read.

Cracking the Code

Dan Brown's *The Da Vinci Code* captivated me from the start. Fast-paced chapters, an intriguing plot, a ticking clock—all of these contributed to a thrilling read. It would be difficult for me to specifically pick out every single TRD in the text because there were so many. Instead I have created a general outline of the major plot characteristics in order to better analyze how they all contributed to the exciting pace.

The book follows multiple perspectives in order to create suspense. It starts with the murder of a curator in Paris, whose death sets off a series of events involving an albino monk, a professor, a police chief, and a cryptologist. The albino monk is established as one of the antagonists who works with a mysterious faction derived from the Roman Catholic Church. His quest is to obtain the Holy Grail. Before the curator died, he left a series of clues behind for the book's major protagonists, Robert Langdon and Sophie Neveu. Sophie warns Robert the police are trying to implicate him in the murder, so they break out of the museum and make themselves fugitives for the rest of the book. The pair uncovers the clues left by the curator and frantically tries to unravel his various codes in a race against time.

Throughout the novel, the characters uncover the truth about the curator's murder and also his secret life in the Priory of Scion. They find themselves plunged into a far-reaching plot much bigger than themselves and involving powerfully sinister forces in the church. After Robert and Sophie swipe a secret *cryptex* (a word coined by Dan Brown) from a Swiss bank, they flee to the estate of Sir Teabing. There Sophie learns the true meaning of the Holy Grail: that Jesus was married to Mary Magdalene, and the church had purposefully destroyed the Gnostic manuscripts in an effort to consolidate its power and create a hierarchal system of authority.

SPOILER ALERT—Robert cleverly defeats Teabing during the climactic scene, saving Sophie, himself, and the secret of the Holy

MASTERING SUSPENSE, STRUCTURE, & PLOT

Grail. The police arrive and exonerate Robert and Sophie, who go on to maintain the secret.

This book works well due to its simplicity and brevity. Brown keeps his chapters short, creating a page-turning sequence. He establishes a "ticking clock" early on and feeds the reader twists and moments of heightened danger on almost a page-by-page basis. This saves the book from becoming merely a weird conspiracy novel.

I've taken his approach into consideration regarding my own novel's chapter lengths. I think in terms of each scene and in what I am trying to accomplish, and then I try to find a way to see it executed in the most interesting, simple, and exciting way possible. Since historical fiction can feel a little too much like a school lecture, a careful balance must be struck. I think Brown's success only underscores the importance of such a balance when writing for contemporary thriller readers. If you want to maintain such a fast pace, you need to integrate many TRDs.

FAQ

Q: My novel focuses on an interracial couple caught in a riot. I know a lot about the couple, how they each got to this point in their lives and where they hope to go from here. My theme is clear to me, too: Ignorance is not bliss. The problem is that I don't know what happens to them after the riot. Now what?

A: Given that character and incident are intimately interwoven, whatever gaps you have when you start to use the tools will close as you work with them. If trying to plot the entire book at once leads to "analysis paralysis," stop for a while and write instead. Think only of the next TRD. Taking this methodical, incremental approach should help you determine what happens next. As Dr. Martin Luther King, Jr. said, "You don't have to see the whole staircase, just take the first step." Your first step is to identify your narrative question: What is your story about? Is it about the riot? Or is the riot a device or a setting to reveal character or to let the characters reveal something important about themselves? If you can answer that one question, you can set off down the highway using Jane's Plotting Road Map.

While I now plot my entire story before I begin to write, I only write to the next TRD. I've found that when I write from plot point to plot point, I'm more focused and efficient than if I try to write without an interim goal. A secondary benefit of using Jane's Plotting Road Map is the confidence it provides. If you feel intimidated or overwhelmed at the prospect of writing an entire book, for example, this tool can be a godsend. Instead of thinking about writing three hundred pages, all you need to focus on is writing five pages or forty pages or seventy pages, a much less daunting task. Further, you'll note that this tactic helps you do more than plot; it also helps you integrate suspense into your plot from the get-go, and the more inherent the suspense, the more harmonious the marriage of character and incident. You'll recall that I determined my thriller should feature a fast pace and my memoir would be better served with a steady pace (Figure 3.2). Figure 3.4 shows how I would start the thriller and plot the memoir, moving, in both cases, from TRD to TRD.

FIGURE 3.4: MAINTAIN A PROPER PACE

CASE STUDY #1: DOMESTIC THRILLER
Approximately p. 5: Kayla runs out of the store to greet the police—and realizes her car has been stolen.
Approximately p. 10: The thief chuckles as he watches Kayla's meltdown from the far side of the grocery store parking lot. He finishes screwing in replacement license plates onto her car, and drives away as Kayla and the police head back into the store.
Approximately p. 15: The police drive Kayla home and conduct a walk-through to confirm no one is inside. She locks every door and window. She reaches for the phone to call her unloved sister, her only nearby family, when she hears her cell phone's distinctive ring tone sounding from somewhere inside the house—the cell phone that had been in her stolen purse.
Approximately p. 20: Kayla calls the police from her neighbor's house. When they arrive, they enter her house with her trailing be-

MASTERING SUSPENSE, STRUCTURE, & PLOT

hind, terrified. The police call her cell phone and locate it in the front hall closet. Inexplicably, it's on the floor.

Approximately p. 25: Kayla's ex-husband tells their ten-year-old daughter that he's sorry she can't see Mommy, that Mommy is a bitch.

Approximately p. 30: The police wait while Kayla packs a few things, and they drive her to her sister's house. Kayla finds the fake rock where her sister has always kept a spare key, but the cubbyhole is empty.

CASE STUDY #2: MEMOIR

Approximately p. 70: Al's wife announces that if he doesn't "man up" and deal with his father and their son, she's leaving him.

Approximately p.140: Al quits his job.

Approximately p. 210: Al confronts his own demons—he's a gambler out of control.

Approximately p. 280: Al gets a new and better job at a community college; his wife agrees to give their marriage another try.

Approximately p. 300: Memoir ends.

FIGURE 3.5: OUTLINING YOUR FIRST TRDS

Now think about the TRDs needed for your project. You know a lot about your book at this point, including the pace you've determined is appropriate. Use Figure 3.5 to outline your first TRDs, adding as many lines as you need.

• Approximately page:
• Approximately page:
• Approximately page:
• Approximately page:
• Approximately page:
• Approximately page:
• Approximately page:

How did the exercise go for you? Were you able to select logical TRDs? As a general rule, the more thinking you do, the better your writing will be, so don't worry if it takes you more time than you expect to complete Figure 3.5. I always spend longer writing my synopses than I do writing my books.

The tools, strategies, and tactics we've discussed thus far will help focus your thinking as you embark on your plotting journey. Before you get too far in, however, don't forget the importance of setting. Deciding where to set your story is the subject of chapter four.

CHAPTER FOUR

SET THE STAGE

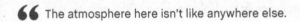

> **"** The atmosphere here isn't like anywhere else. **"**
>
> —JOHN CENA

CHARACTER- OR INCIDENT-DRIVEN DECISION MAKING

The most common way to create suspense is to let your reader share a character's anxiety. It's absorbing to follow a character who knows something bad is going to happen, especially if the details—the where and when and what—aren't revealed right away. It's the anticipation that's the killer. Maybe someone is chasing you or stalking you or threatening you. You're looking over your shoulder as you stumble toward a place you hope is safe. There's a sense of foreboding that haunts your every move and builds with every step. Certain settings lend themselves to building this kind of fearsome suspense: Think of yourself alone, after dark, in a deserted cemetery with someone chasing you. Fog swirls around the tombstones.

Donald Bain, who collaborated with his wife, Renée Paley-Bain, and the fictional Jessica Fletcher, used this technique in 2014's *Death of a Blue Blood*, the forty-second book in the *USA Today* best-selling Murder, She Wrote mystery series. After a lady's maid is found murdered in the garden, Jessica (the protagonist) finds herself alone on the grounds of a Gothic-era castle deep in the picturesque British countryside when she hears a twig snap followed by inexplicably rustling leaves. Someone, Jessica realizes, is there, moving stealthily toward her. You're there, in the garden, with a protagonist you care about. You're sharing the anxious moment.

This suspense-building tactic is reliable and reader friendly. When taking this approach, however, you need to ensure that the incident derives from a character's personality trait or from the situation; otherwise, you risk having the scene feel clichéd or trite. Jessica's presence is credible because of her repute as a best-selling author. She didn't wander into an aristocratic party; her British publisher arranged an invitation. Knowing Jessica's backstory ensures that her presence at the estate feels logical, not manufactured.

This sense of rightness doesn't merely apply to exotic or dramatic situations. Your settings must include only the kinds of places your character would go. Let's say you have a character who is revealed to be depressed in the first chapter; her only solace is hiking. A hundred pages later, when that woman is told to get herself together by a mean-spirited, know-it-all cousin, she retreats into herself and, as soon as she can, escapes onto a nearby hiking trail. When a feral dog attacks her, your readers won't find her presence in the woods contrived—you've previously planted the seed that makes her current reaction seem inevitable.

MASTERING SUSPENSE, STRUCTURE, & PLOT

What you don't want to do is have a woman who is all alone in a haunted manor house hear chains clanking overhead and decide not to wait for the police, but to investigate by herself. As she starts up the steps to the attic, your readers will shout, "Don't go up the stairs!" as they roll their eyes.

While character must dictate behavior and thus locale, you don't necessarily need to start with character. You can plot first, then retrofit character traits and behaviors to suit that action. For instance, in *Killer Keepsakes*, the fourth Josie Prescott Antiques Mystery, I needed to add an element of danger (a TRD) around page 280. I decided to burn down someone's condo. I set the condo on a serene pond, with ducks and lush vegetation, a pleasing juxtaposition to fear and man-made destruction. In order for Josie to have an organic reason for being on scene and available to help save a life, I needed to go back and make the condo owner, one of Josie's employees, sick. Josie, being Josie, brings a bouquet of get-well flowers. Josie's character is established and consistent—it is unsurprising that she would be in that place at that time.

The key to success is to align your suspenseful moments with previously introduced character traits. Figure 4.1 shows you how to think through this process.

FIGURE 4.1: ALIGN CHARACTER ATTRIBUTES AND SETTINGS

PERSONALITY TRAIT: Gullible

BEHAVIOR IMPLICATION: Trusting of strangers

SETTING IMPLICATION: Seemingly chance encounters might occur at parties, train stations, etc. The more activity swirls around your character, the less noticeable his or her random connection will be.

PERSONALITY TRAIT: Insecure

BEHAVIOR IMPLICATION: Compensates with swagger

SETTING IMPLICATION: A place where people of genuine substance gather will intimidate your character. If he is a doctor, he'd feel awkward at a conference where other doctors are presenting scholarly papers, while he's merely a member of the audience; if she is a stay-at-home mom, attending one of her children's classmate's birthday parties, the hosting mom presenting a Martha Stewart-worthy cake with a self-satisfied flourish would make her feel inferior.

PERSONALITY TRAIT: Lazy

BEHAVIOR IMPLICATION: Manipulates people

SETTING IMPLICATION: Any location where he's expected to work. A charming young man might convince a vulnerable young woman to complete his paperwork. A teenager addicted to video games might persuade his mother to let him skip his chores. Think Tom Sawyer and the whitewashed fence.

PERSONALITY TRAIT: Altruistic

BEHAVIOR IMPLICATION: Thinks of other people first

SETTING IMPLICATION: The site of charitable good works, like a church bazaar or a charity auction.

PERSONALITY TRAIT: Narcissistic

BEHAVIOR IMPLICATION: Enjoys watching other people suffer or lose out (schadenfreude)

SETTING IMPLICATION: A place where your character's accomplishments allow him or her to gloat

ADAPTING A GOTHIC NOVEL

Gothic fiction, a genre that can trace its roots to Horace Walpole's 1764 novel, *The Castle of Otranto*, became wildly popular in the nineteenth century and is still in fashion today. The term derives from the setting these novels typically embrace—old castles on bleak moors, for instance, or ruinous mansions set in isolated locations, like a mountain retreat accessible only when the snow melts or a deserted leper colony hidden behind a rusted metal fence. The setting becomes a stage on which the action occurs, the sinister milieu supplying titillating terror.

In Emily Brontë's mid-nineteenth century novel, *Wuthering Heights*, for example, the gloomy and baleful environ sets the tone of the novel as vividly as if a Greek chorus stood nearby, mouthing words of impending doom. The setting communicates attitude and intention in the same way a character would.

Similarly, Dennis Lehane created a gothic ethos in his 2003 novel *Shutter Island*. Set in a hospital for the criminally insane located on a desolate island, the environment reflects the inhabitants' situations. No one needs to describe the loneliness of that forsaken place, the ominous miasma hanging over it, or the despondency of the inmates; the setting itself does the talking. The setting is a metaphor that adds layers of meaning to the story.

While the role of the setting in gothic and gothic-like novels is apparent, all stories, whether fiction or narrative nonfiction, need to include settings that support the underlying themes, thus adding verisimilitude to the action.

LESS IS MORE

Early novels tended to include lengthy geographic depictions that many of today's readers would consider interminably drawn out and downright boring. Those writers appropriately painted pictures of places few readers would ever see. Today, with the advent of television and the Internet, even dedicated armchair travelers have different expectations than readers of generations past. Contemporary readers don't want labored descriptions of hills and valleys and beaches and cityscapes; they want to read about experiences that could occur only at that place during that time. You should integrate only those details needed to bring the incidents you're writing about to life. As you read the excerpt from Hank Phillippi Ryan's award-winning novel, *The Other Woman*, notice how little exposition is needed to create suspense.

"Get that light out of my face! And get behind the tape. All of you. *Now.*" Detective Jake Brogan pointed his own flashlight at the pack of reporters, its cold glow highlighting one news-greedy face after another in the October darkness. He recognized television. Radio. That kid from the paper. *How the hell did they get here so fast?* The whiffle of a chopper, one of theirs, hovered over the riverbank, its spotlights illuminating the unmistakable—another long night on the job. And a Monday-morning visit to a grieving family. If they could figure out who this victim was.

A body by the river. This time, the Charles, down by the old dock. Her legs, black tights striped with mud, leather boots, one zipper down, splayed on the fallen leaves and slimy underbrush on the bank. Her head, chestnut hair floating like a punk Ophelia, bobbing and grotesque in the tangled weeds.

Too bad I can't call Jane. She'd love this.

Jake's yellow beam of light landed on that Tucker kid, notebook out and edging toward the body. Rubber boots squished in the muck of the riverbank, still soft from Boston's run of bad-luck weather. "Hey, you. *Out.* This means you. You don't wanna have to call your new editor to *bail* you out."

"Is it a serial killer?" A reporter's voice thin and reedy, carried in the chill wind. The neon green from the Boston Garden billboards, the purple beacons decorating the white-cabled Zakim Bridge, the glaring yellow of the chopper's spots colored the crime scene into a B-movie carnival.

"Are you calling it a serial killing? You think it's one person? Was she killed the same way as the other?"

"Yeah, tell us, Jake," another voice demanded. "Is two murders serial?"

"One a couple weeks ago, one today, that's two." A different reporter's voice. "Both women. Both by water. By bridges. Both weekend nights. Both dead. That's serial. We're going with that. Maybe . . . 'the River Killer.' "

"We are, too. The Bridge Killer."

"Have you figured out who the first victim is?"

"Outta here, all of you!"

Jake tucked his flashlight under one arm, zipped his Boston Po-lice-issue brown leather jacket. Reporters scrambling to nickname a murderer. Crazy. *What does Jane always say? It bleeds, it leads?* At least her stories aren't like that.

A siren screamed across Causeway Street; then the red-striped ambulance careened down the rutted side street. Every camera turned to the EMTs scrambling out the opening ambulance doors.

No need for them to hurry, Jake thought. His watch showed 2:15 A.M. She'd been dead for at least three hours.

Just like the other woman.

CHOOSING SETTINGS BASED ON GENRE

Different genres come with different reader expectations that pertain to setting. For instance, readers expect cozies to be set in small towns and hard-boiled detective stories to be based in cities. In some genres, such as fantasy, world building is crucial. For instance, if you're writing a novel about an underwater civilization, you might do the following:

- Integrate challenging terrain, such as caverns and mountain ranges to enable your characters to showcase their athleti-cism, bravery, or wit.
- Create longing through juxtaposition by featuring a man who yearns to live on dry land and allow him access to a sand bar where he can see grass and forests, his dream so close, and yet so far away.
- Invent societal systems that are consistent and logical, and develop characters who understand how those systems op-erate—a kind of pecking order, perhaps, that allows warriors to inhabit the deeper environs, relegating the rest of society to the less desirable surface areas.

In other genres, like historical fiction, readers want to be immersed in the period not only to see what was there and what wasn't, but to experience how people lived. In Diana Gabaldon's *New York Times* #1 bestseller *Outlander,* the Scottish Highlands come alive with lush descriptions—but these descriptions occur only as characters interact with the environment.

While in the Scottish Highlands in 1945, Claire touches a stone in a circular henge and is mysteriously transported back to 1743. Marrying historical romance to time travel, the events feel contemporary. The fields of heather, the craggy rocks, the dark castles, the mysterious stones, every element evokes a sense of time and place. The book runs to 850 pages, yet because the focus is on incident, not description, the enduringly popular novel is considered a fast read.

Contemporary romance readers also expect settings to transport them to another world. Readers of this genre crave the entire romance package, not simply a love story. They want to vicariously experience a grand romance. They don't want merely to walk down the Champs-Élysées in Paris—that's a place they know well (in their imaginations) from the countless books, movies, and television shows that feature it. They want a unique experience. Take them someplace they can't go on their own, like an appointment at the American Embassy in Paris or a party at the Ambassador's residence. Don't merely send them into the National Gallery of Art in London; let them sit in on a curatorial meeting with the Queen's archivist. Don't make them sit passively on the outside patio at Bangkok's Peninsula Hotel, or if you do, be certain they see something remarkable, like a woman in in a tight black dress and stiletto heels jumping onto a commuter boat traveling along the Chao Phraya River. Readers would rather go on an elephant ride through the jungle outside Bangkok or get a sexy soapy massage in the Huay Kwang section of the city than sit quietly in a hotel room. When writing unusual locations, go big.

This principle isn't unique to romance readers. All readers want to spend time in settings they don't know, or settings that, while familiar, are freshly envisioned. Consider John Cheever's 1964 short story, "The Swimmer," a retelling of the Greek myth of Narcissus. Narcissus, you'll recall, died staring at his own reflection shimmering in a pool of water. In "The Swimmer," which was originally published in *The New Yorker*, Cheever used his trademark suburban setting to make observations about social status, wealth, and self-aggrandizement. As the story becomes increasingly surreal, readers' perceptions of suburbia darken.

OPPOSITES ATTRACT

Sometimes you want to choose a setting that contrasts with your character's longing or your story's conflict. For instance, consider how intriguing these paradoxical pairings might be.

- A romance between a convicted killer and a lonely woman. Their searing love affair develops in a dingy prison visiting room under a guard's watchful eye.
- A memoir focusing on a woman's dramatic rise from poverty and homelessness to the corporate boardroom. The first time she goes home after reaching this pinnacle of success, she visits an old school chum who now lives in a desolate trailer park.

Choosing settings that contrast with your characters' situations adds spice to your stories, highlighting your thematic underpinnings by encouraging readers to think about the deep issues in your stories.

Judith Guest's 1976 novel, *Ordinary People,* also focuses on an affluent suburban family. The nondistinctive environment—the kind of upper-middle-class suburban oasis found in all fifty states—casts the extraordinary events into sharp relief. This idealized family is ripped apart when the eldest son, Buck, is killed in a sailing accident. Conrad, the younger son, survives. *Ordinary People* follows the three remaining members of the family, Conrad and his parents, as they come to terms with their loss. The book is written in the third-person omniscient voice, in the present tense, with chapters alternating between the surviving son, Conrad, and his father, Calvin. Dealing with themes of life and death, survival and suicide, trust and betrayal, this work of literary fiction uses its affluent location as a counterpoint to the desolate emotions the characters must confront.

Aligning your setting with your theme adds engaging complexity to your story. As you read through the listings in Figure 4.2, note how the settings help support the authors' themes.

FIGURE 4.2: ALIGN SETTINGS WITH THEMES

TITLE/AUTHOR/YEAR OF PUBLICATION: *Black Mountain*, Rex Stout, 1954

GENRE: Crime fiction

THEME(S): Without love, there can be no loyalty.

SETTING: The rugged, foreboding terrain at and near the Black Mountain in Montenegro

RELATIONSHIP OF THEME TO SETTING: The detectives, being Americans, are free to love as they choose; the victim's relatives, being oppressed by a totalitarian government, cannot. The difficulties the detectives must endure proves their commitment to solving the crime and demonstrates their love for the victim.

TITLE/AUTHOR/YEAR OF PUBLICATION: *Not Without My Daughter*, Betty Mahmoody with William Hoffer, 1987

GENRE: Memoir

THEME(S): Escaping tyranny for the love of a child—and the love of oneself

SETTING: Tehran (Iran) and the mountainous region between Tehran and Turkey

RELATIONSHIP OF THEME TO SETTING: Examples highlight the cultural differences that drive the protagonist to escape. For instance, her daughter attends a school that begs for donations so they can install toilets before the academic year begins; they raise enough money and are thrilled with the new holes in the ground. The dangerous precipices and icy conditions along their escape route mirror the dangers the protagonist would face if she were caught.

TITLE/AUTHOR/YEAR OF PUBLICATION: *The Blank Wall*, Elisabeth Sanxay Holding, 1947

GENRE: Psychological thriller

THEME(S): A mother's love is unconditional.

SETTING: A house on a lake in a suburb of New York City

RELATIONSHIP OF THEME TO SETTING: The house and grounds, including the lake and a small island, are the totality of the protagonist's life. She doesn't aspire to more. As she loses control of the situation (the unexplained death of her teenage daughter's much older, bad boy boyfriend), the familiarity of her universe serves as both a sanctuary and a prison.

TITLE/AUTHOR/YEAR OF PUBLICATION: *China Dolls*, Lisa See, 2014

GENRE: Literary fiction

THEME(S): You need girlfriends more than you need family; be careful whom you trust.

SETTING: San Francisco, starting in 1938

RELATIONSHIP OF THEME TO SETTING: The three Chinese women who are the "dolls" in this story meet by accident at a nightclub. They come from wildly different backgrounds and circumstances. The kaleidoscopic diversity, ethnic ghettos, and rampant optimism of prewar San Francisco provide a telling backdrop for this complex story.

TITLE/AUTHOR/YEAR OF PUBLICATION: *A Spool of Blue Thread*, Anne Tyler, 2015

GENRE: Women's fiction

THEME(S): Every family, no matter how seemingly ordinary, is special.

SETTING: Baltimore, spanning multiple generations

RELATIONSHIP OF THEME TO SETTING: The family home, a sprawling symbol of stability and endurance

SENSUAL REFERENCES BRING YOUR SETTING TO LIFE

After you've determined what your suspenseful setting looks like, it's time to write. The more sensual references you integrate, the more heightened the suspense. Whether the suspenseful moment is action orientated (e.g., a ghoulish creature chasing your protagonist through the deserted streets of an urban wasteland, drawing ever closer) or psychological (e.g., a country kitchen where an apparently kind woman's barbed criticisms grow ever darker), your readers will feel more present if they can experience the situation as if they're in the scene themselves. Figure 4.3 details an approach to writing your suspenseful settings. Getting your thoughts in order before you put pen to paper ensures your description will enliven the scene, not slow it down.

FIGURE 4.3: A SENSUAL APPROACH TO CREATING SETTINGS

GENRE: Young adult horror

YOUR PROTAGONIST: A seventeen-year-old boy, evidently, the only survivor of a cataclysmic attack by the ghouls. His name is John.

BRIEFLY DESCRIBE THE SCENE: A ghoul spots John and tries to capture him. John flees, darting into back alleys, running up deserted staircases, and finally jumping into an old, empty water main tunnel system, a place the ghoul can't follow. (Ghouls don't go underground.)

TYPE OF SUSPENSE: Action: A ghoul chasing John through the deserted streets of an urban wasteland, drawing ever closer

WHAT IS YOUR PROTAGONIST LONGING FOR? Short-term: safety; long-term: help; emotionally: to know he's not alone

WHAT IS YOUR THEME? We're all alone; only you can save yourself.

WHAT DOES YOUR PROTAGONIST HEAR? Whooshes, cackling laughs, his own labored breathing, pounding footsteps

---

WHAT DOES YOUR PROTAGONIST SEE? A green fluorescent haze emanating from the creature that glows brighter as it gains on him; rhomboids of silver moonlight; dark buildings; barren streets

WHAT DOES YOUR PROTAGONIST SMELL? The stench of the garbage lying in uncollected heaps along the curb; the cloyingly sweet aroma of hibiscus as John runs by the planters sitting in front of a now-deserted apartment building

WHAT DOES YOUR PROTAGONIST TASTE? The last bite of a ham sandwich John swallowed before running for his life

WHAT IS YOUR PROTAGONIST TOUCHING? The hard asphalt, his jeans as John rubs his sweating palms against the rough fabric

WHAT IS YOUR PROTAGONIST EXPERIENCING PHYSIOLOGICALLY? Twisted steel-like tension in his neck and shoulders; his raging pulse

WHAT IS YOUR PROTAGONIST EXPERIENCING EMOTIONALLY? Fear, but not panic; determination

GENRE: Memoir

YOUR PROTAGONIST: A middle-aged woman trying to come to terms with her mother's snide contempt. The protagonist is Mary. Her mother is Joan.

BRIEFLY DESCRIBE THE SCENE: Mary comes to Joan's house for her monthly duty call. Joan bakes bread. They have coffee. The conversation starts out chatty and inconsequential, but Joan, as always, finds ways to criticize without openly doing so. Mary stands up while Joan is still talking, says she has to go, and leaves.

TYPE OF SUSPENSE: Psychological: A country kitchen where Joan's barbed criticisms grow ever darker

WHAT IS YOUR PROTAGONIST LONGING FOR? Short-term: to escape Joan's kitchen unscathed; long-term: to never feel judged by Joan again; emotionally: to know she doesn't need her mother's approval to thrive

WHAT IS YOUR THEME? You need to judge yourself by your own standards, not someone else's.

WHAT DOES YOUR PROTAGONIST HEAR? The soft whirr of the refrigerator cycling on and off, a barking dog somewhere in the distance, coffee perking

WHAT DOES YOUR PROTAGONIST SEE? Joan's crimped gray hair, trembling hands, and smile that doesn't reach her hard brown eyes;

a set of red canisters that have been on the counter since Mary was a girl; chipped paint that Mary never before noticed

WHAT DOES YOUR PROTAGONIST SMELL? Cinnamon and vanilla from baking cinnamon buns, aromas Mary used to associate with love, but now represent contempt; bleach

WHAT DOES YOUR PROTAGONIST TASTE? An acrid, bitter aftertaste, which Mary doesn't recognize as adrenaline; to her it's simply a by-product of stepping into the house where she was reared

WHAT IS YOUR PROTAGONIST TOUCHING? The satiny smooth oak table; a splinter from the old ladder-back chair

WHAT IS YOUR PROTAGONIST EXPERIENCING PHYSIOLOGICALLY? Nausea; a kind of dullness that makes concentration hard

WHAT IS YOUR PROTAGONIST EXPERIENCING EMOTIONALLY? Dread that she won't be able to escape her mother's web

FIGURE 4.4: THINK DEEPLY ABOUT YOUR SETTING

This exercise will help you create vivid and suspenseful scenes by paying careful attention to your settings and how your characters interact with the world around them. Once you identify the mood you want to create, you need to determine which details will allow your readers to feel as if they're in that place at that moment. Those are the ones to include. Those are the ones that will keep readers engaged in your story.

- What's your genre?
- Briefly describe the scene.
- Who is your protagonist?
- What is your protagonist longing for?
- What is your theme?
- What is your plot goal?
- Do you hope to achieve suspense through action or psychology?
- What does your protagonist see?
- What does your protagonist hear?

- What does your protagonist smell?
- What does your protagonist taste?
- What is your protagonist touching?
- What is your protagonist experiencing physiologically?
- What is your protagonist experiencing emotionally?

Whatever settings you choose, they need to align with your theme, support the plot, and help define your characters. This idea of people interacting with places provides rich opportunities for subtle and deep engagement.

FAQ

Q: I'm writing a middle school novel about a group of preteen orphans who live in a long-forgotten tunnel system under Central Park in New York City. The tunnel system is an urban legend. No one knows if it's true. I think I need to devote at least one chapter to describing the tunnels. Otherwise I'll have to keep interrupting action scenes to explain things. How can I avoid an info dump in that first chapter?

A: I understand the temptation to start off with a description of your setting, especially since it's unique, but it is always better to let the action do the talking. When one of your protagonists charges down a long stretch of tunnel, that's the time to let the reader see it. But even then, don't describe it. Instead of writing that the concrete had grayed with age, have your young orphan feel cocky that he knows the twists and turns so well he could run through them blindfolded, whereas his pursuer had better keep his eyes peeled. *Ha!* the orphan might think. *With any luck he'll smack flat into a wall and knock himself out.* Your challenge is the same as that faced by every author—include only those details necessary for the story or that inform character.

Consider this description from Rex Stout's 1954 Nero Wolfe detective novel, *Black Mountain*. As you read this excerpt, note how little description Stout provided. Instead he used incident to reveal setting. In the process, we learn more about the narrator, Archie Goodwin.

Archie is recounting a leg of their European journey as they hunt for the killer of Mr. Wolfe's oldest and best friend. Wolfe and Goodwin have met with a group of men high in the Montenegro mountains. After a difficult trek and sleeping in near-freezing conditions, they need to cross the border into Albania where they'll face certain danger. The following excerpt is from chapter twelve, about two-thirds of the way through the book.

> It wasn't until the knapsacks were strapped on and we were ready to go that I realized we would have to return to the trail by way of the ledge. Numb and dumb with cold, I had been supposing that we would go on to the border without any backtracking. With seven pairs of eyes on me, not counting Wolfe's, it was up to me to sustain the honor of American manhood, and I set my jaw and did my best. It helped that my back was to them. An interesting question about walking a narrow ledge over a 1,500-foot drop is whether it's better to do it at night or in the daytime. My answer is that it's better not to do it at all.

You can feel the cold—it's in Archie's bones. You can feel the fear—and you learn something important about Archie as we witness him rise above it. You admire his wit. And you see the geography. As Mr. Stout did in *Black Mountain*, show the characters interacting with their world; don't rely on exposition.

PEOPLE INTERACTING WITH PLACES

One of the themes in my Josie Prescott Antiques Mysteries is finding community. Josie, after losing her job, her friends, her boyfriend, and her dad, all within a few months, decides to move to Rocky Point, New Hampshire, to start a new life. New Hampshire's rugged coastline and long, hard winters contrast sharply with the theme, allowing me to write about places that bridge the gap between theme and place. Consider this excerpt from 2016's *Glow of Death*:

> Frills of white caps and sun-sparked opalescent sequins dotted the dark blue ocean. Rocky Point, New Hampshire, was beautiful in all seasons, from the fiery colors of autumn to the pristine whites of winter to the red buds and unfurled green leaves of spring, but it

was summer I liked the most. The wild grasses on the sandy dunes. The buttercups and honeysuckle. The easy breezes. I was a sucker for a breeze.

Rather than simply describing Rocky Point, I let my readers see it through Josie's eyes.

In Isak Dinesen's 1938 novel, *Out of Africa*, the narrator starts with a description of the farm where the protagonist lives. The exposition goes on for more than 3,500 words (more than ten pages) before we come to some dialogue. The narration is written in the first person, so while it might be cumbersome for today's readers, you are able to see what the protagonist sees, such as trees that are different from those found in Europe. That reflection occurs in the second paragraph of the novel, and from that singular comment, we garner important information about the character. This technique—slipping backstory into descriptions of setting by letting your readers experience the place alongside your character—is one of the best ways to let your readers in on your character's secrets, opinions, heritage, longings, and intentions.

Now that you know where your story takes place and how to write about it experientially, it's time to weave in two subplots, the subject of chapter five.

CHAPTER FIVE

LAYER IN TWO SUBPLOTS

> " The art of simplicity is a puzzle of complexity. "
>
> —DOUGLAS HORTON

SUBPLOTS WITH PURPOSE

You'll recall from chapter three that Jane's Plotting Road Map includes two service roads: Service Road #1 and Service Road #2 (abbreviated as SR1 and SR2). In most traditionally plotted books, you want to select two subplots and insert a scene relating to one of them every forty pages or so, alternating between them. At the end, the three plotlines will come together, infusing your conclusion with layers of tantalizing complexity. Without subplots, your story may feel too simple and linear. Selecting subplots can be thorny, however. You need to ensure the subplot supports your primary plot, adding intrigue and interest without distracting your readers—this is not easy.

Before you decide on a subplot, determine its purpose. The two most common reasons to integrate subplots are to add intricacy to your primary plot and to develop situations that reveal nuanced information about your characters. For instance, you can introduce a new character, changing perspective and/or point of view; this character will, at some point, interact with your protagonist. Likewise, you could show your protagonist engaged in a hobby, say whittling. In order to whittle well, one must be patient and focused and have steady hands. Later, when your protagonist is aiming a rifle at the bad guy in a raging snowstorm, waiting for him to come out from behind a tree, your readers will accept the character's ability to be patient, to focus, and to remain steady without question. How the character feels about whittling (and how the other people in his life feel about his spending time this way), what he produces, whether he shares his work—all these myriad issues are fodder for the subplot. Perhaps he thinks of himself as a novice and never lets anyone see anything, then at the end of the book, he gives the young girl he's rescued an object he's been working on throughout the story. Linking your subplots to your primary plot—that's the key to storytelling success.

FAQ

Q: How many subplots are too many?

A: While some stories merit more than two subplots, most do not. For instance, if you're writing a sweeping family saga, various minor characters might need a voice to tell their part of the story, and allowing them to do so will add resonance to the plot. That's an unusual situation, though, and you need to consider carefully before adding more than two. What you don't want to do is confuse your readers. Confusion occurs when one subplot gets more attention than the others, yet isn't actually worthy of that attention. This inappropriate accentuation often occurs because the author gets interested in the secondary plot and loses sight of its plot-driving or character-revealing purpose. From your readers' points of view, they're following along, caught up in the story, wondering with delight how this subplot will figure into the main action, and when it doesn't play a significant role, they feel let down, misled, and maybe even gypped.

This idea of choosing subplots for a specific purpose is foreign to some authors. These writers get interested in a character, perhaps, and allow that character to play a larger role than they'd originally intended, calling the new narrative a subplot. Often, however, the result is a distraction that merely slows the pace. We can learn from one of President Abraham Lincoln's favorite riddles: If you call a dog's tail a leg, how many legs does it have? His answer: Four. Just because you call a tail a leg doesn't make it a leg. Just because you call a digression a subplot doesn't make it a subplot. Subplots should only be included if they serve a specific plot- or character-building purpose. Consider these scenarios in which you're highlighting a particular characteristic (knowledge or goodness, for instance) or complicating the plot (circling around an issue or adding in suspects):

- If your novel is about the slow disintegration of a marriage, perhaps you want to showcase your protagonist as a loving dad. You could create a subplot highlighting how it is he who rescues his son from some kind of trouble, while all his wife does is fret and blame him and wallow. This approach creates instant and sustained sympathy for the husband.
- Many readers report they love learning new things. One of the most effective ways to integrate information that will engage your readers' interest throughout the book is by adding a subplot. A doctor, for instance, could treat a patient with a mysterious ailment. While that particular patient has nothing to do with your primary plot, the doctor's persis-

MASTERING SUSPENSE, STRUCTURE, & PLOT

tence and dedication and kindness do. Later, when the doctor behaves in a similar manner while doing something that relates to the story's core, readers will find it credible. The subplot serves a dual purpose: Readers learn unexpected tidbits about diagnostic methodology, satisfying their desire to learn new things, and you showcase relevant qualities about the doctor, adding credibility and reducing the likelihood that someone will find a later plot point coincidental or contrived.

- In a memoir, small incidents add up to big themes. Let's say a single mother recounts her struggles to get her seventeen-year-old son the car he needs for his after-school job. A subplot mirroring the financial hardship takes an incident and converts it into a theme. For instance, a logical subplot might involve her father, who also needs financial assistance. Over the course of the book, his needs grow more acute. She's in a quandary. She has enough money to help one of them, but not both. She's torn, and she must make a choice. Or, the subplot could focus on something that is opposite to her current situation. Maybe she has a cousin who is wealthy and she needs to overcome the embarrassment natural to a forty-five-year-old woman who finds herself having to ask for financial help; that would serve as an intriguing counterpoint to the primary story point—rearing her son to be independent, and here she is, dependent. To really grind home the dilemma, perhaps her cousin stops by to show off her new car.
- Police procedurals often feature a flawed hero, like a cop with an alcohol problem. That problem becomes a subplot, which, if handled well, places the detective in situations that show whether he has the issue under control or doesn't.

Note how each of these subplot examples resulted from thoughtful consideration. None are random or unrelated to the primary plot or protagonist. Choose subplots to highlight key facts, add complexity to your characters, and build suspense, and you'll stay in your lane. Don't ramble or go off on tangents because you think the detour is a subplot; it's not. Pretending otherwise is a surefire way to reach a dead end.

MAXIMIZE YOUR SUBPLOTS' POTENTIAL

Your subplots should do the following:

- Include fully developed plotlines
- Feature fully developed characters
- Reveal attributes of your main characters that otherwise wouldn't be shown
- Be resolved by the end of the story, either before the main plot is revealed or simultaneously
- Mirror your overarching themes or contradict them
- Never overtake your primary plot

Selecting subplots that contribute to page-turning suspense requires thought and care. Take a look at Figure 5.1 to see how this versatile tool—a subplot—seamlessly adds information about characters and/or intrigue to plots.

FIGURE 5.1: SUBPLOTS WITH PURPOSE

GENRE: Literary fiction

PLOT AND SUBPLOT EXAMPLE: Philip Roth's 1959 novella, *Goodbye, Columbus*, was first published in *The Paris Review*. The primary plot revolves around the romance between Neil, a lower-middle-class Jew with a low-paying job at a library, and Brenda, a wealthy Jew, studying at Radcliff. (The book of the same name, which contained five short stories in addition to the novella, won the 1960 National Book Award.) Neil lives in a blue-collar neighborhood of Newark, New Jersey. Brenda is from Short Hills, an affluent suburb. The theme of the novella is assimilation and its effect on individuality. A subplot featuring an

African-American child who loves art books mirrors the primary plot, adding depth, interest, and thought-provoking reflections.

SUBPLOT'S PURPOSE: To mirror a character's dilemma

GENRE: Fantasy

PLOT AND SUBPLOT EXAMPLE: J.R.R. Tolkien's series, The Lord of Rings, first published in 1954, follows Frodo's quest to destroy the One Ring. An important secondary plot revolves around Legolas Greenleaf and Aragorn's adventures as they strive to protect settlements and destroy Orc armies. Other subplots also focus on polarities including optimism and despair, mortality and athanasia, and predetermination and free will.

SUBPLOT'S PURPOSE: To highlight goodness by showing evil

GENRE: Memoir

PLOT AND SUBPLOT EXAMPLE: World-famous neurologist Oliver Sacks's 2015 memoir, *On the Move*, tracks his experiences as a lover of motorcycles and a chronicler of neurological anomalies. A subplot discusses another aspect of his life: sex. A by-product perhaps of his shy nature and deeply religious upbringing, his intense yet infrequent sexual relationships serve as a counterpoint for his ever-present and public work.

SUBPLOT'S PURPOSE: To understand the role sex played in his life

GENRE: Traditional Mystery

PLOT AND SUBPLOT EXAMPLE: In *Killer Keepsakes*, the fourth book in the Josie Prescott Antiques Mystery series, Gretchen, Josie's gregarious and dependable assistant, goes missing. When a corpse is found in Gretchen's condo, she's the chief suspect. Uncovering layers of secrets about Gretchen's past, Josie learns about shocking abuse that Gretchen endured for years. A subplot focuses on the true story of Henrietta Howard, a gentry-born, eighteenth-century British woman. Henrietta survived an abusive marriage and reinvented herself as a member of Princess Caroline's staff, and after spending years as the mistress to King George II, Henrietta went on to become one of the most sought-after women of her generation, friend of the greatest poets and intellectuals of her day.

SUBPLOT'S PURPOSE: To mirror the primary plot—with will and grit, you can reinvent yourself.

USE JANE'S PLOTTING ROAD MAP TO ENSURE YOU MAINTAIN A SUSPENSEFUL PACE

Don't squander the suspense-building capability of subplots. When you make them meaty, they add complexity and intrigue. We've been working on two case studies, a thriller and a memoir. As you read through the subplot story points detailed in Figure 5.2, note how they accentuate different aspects of a situation or a person, weaving together unexpected threads to make a vibrant tapestry. Also note how I'm estimating that some aspect of each subplot will occur every eighty pages or so, starting around page forty. (SR1 will come into play on pages 40, 120, 200, 280, etc. SR2 will come into play on pages 80, 160, 240, 320, etc.) This tempo may vary, of course, depending on the main story's pace and the plot point's significance.

FIGURE 5.2: WEAVE IN SUBPLOTS

CASE STUDY #1: DOMESTIC THRILLER

BEGINNING: Kayla reaches for a box of cereal in her suburban grocery store. When she turns back to her cart, she discovers that her purse is gone.

THRILLER SUBPLOT #1: Kayla's mom has Sundown Syndrome, evening-onset dementia.

- **Approximately p. 40:** As Kayla is pouring herself a glass of wine after finishing a long and frightening conversation with the police, her mother calls to complain that her housekeeper stole her red silk blouse. Kayla calls the housekeeper, a woman named Ada who's worked for her mom for eight years. Ada says of course she didn't steal the blouse, that the blouse is at the dry cleaners, and that she thinks her mom is getting dotty.
- **Approximately p. 120:** Kayla arranges with a visiting nurse service to conduct a safety audit on her mom's behalf. Her mom refuses to cooperate, sitting outside in a lawn chair the whole time. The nurse assessor tells Kayla that her mom is not taking

MASTERING SUSPENSE, STRUCTURE, & PLOT

her medication properly. Her mom calls the assessor a crackpot out to hook a customer for their visiting nurse services.

- **Approximately p. 200:** Kayla's mom seems happier than she has in years. She confides that it's that nice young man who's been helping her since Ada left. Kayla, stunned at the dual turn of events, calls Ada who reports her mother fired her last week. Kayla is appalled and offers Ada severance and a letter of reference. Her mom refuses to tell her anything about why she fired Ada or the new man, saying she knows Kayla would chase him off because she doesn't want her to have any pleasure in her life. Kayla asks her mother to sign a power of attorney; she refuses.

- **Approximately p. 280:** Kayla sneaks a nanny-cam into her mother's house and is shocked to see that the "nice young man" is her ex-husband, Bill. She calls and reads him the riot act. He tells her to take a chill pill, that he and her mom are pals, and hangs up.

- **Approximately p. 360:** Kayla gets a call from the hospital near her mom. A gardener working on one of her mother's neighbor's houses found her mom in the bushes at 7 A.M. Her mom was asleep. The gardener called 911.

- **At the end:** Kayla convinces her mother to go into assisted living. Kayla says, "Think about it, Ma. If you didn't have to spend so much time and energy coping, think of what you could accomplish."

THRILLER SUBPLOT #2: Kayla's ex-husband is stalking her.

- **Approximately p. 80:** Kayla's ex-husband, Bill, calls to let her know he's getting remarried. Kayla can't tell if he wanted to make sure she heard the news from him like he said, or whether he's bragging as she suspects.

- **Approximately p. 160:** Bill shows up at Kayla's job saying he wants to talk about the money he owes her. She steps outside with him and he gives his famous quirky grin and says he lied—he just wanted to see her. She runs inside and hides in the ladies' room until a co-worker tells her he's gone.

- **Approximately p. 240:** Kayla sees Bill in his idling car down the block from her house. She calls the police, and a detective brings Bill in for questioning.

- **Approximately p. 320:** Kayla sees Bill twice, both times lurking just out of sight. She calls her lawyer to file for sole custody of the kids.

- **At the end:** Kayla closes the door on her house for the last time, ready to start her new life. Before walking down the pathway, she looks around, and when she doesn't see Bill, she smiles.

CASE STUDY #2: MEMOIR

BEGINNING: Al sits in his home office waiting for a reply to the text he just sent his sister. Their dad is refusing to get out of bed—again. The phone rings. It's the police. His teenage son Stewart has been arrested—again.

MEMOIR SUBPLOT #1: Al has a gambling problem.

- **Approximately p. 40:** Al attends a neighborhood poker party and loses $120.
- **Approximately p. 120:** Al leaves work early to join a craps game. He wins $750.
- **Approximately p. 200:** Al gets so involved in what was supposed to be a quick lunchtime poker game he misses a meeting with his boss, the school principal.
- **Approximately p. 280:** Al takes his neighbor, Sheila, to a nearby casino. They stay so late that they're exhausted by the time they leave. Al falls asleep at the wheel and drives into a tree, totaling his car.
- **Approximately p. 360:** Al joins Gambler's Anonymous.
- **At the end:** Al walks past his neighbor's house where the men are sitting around the card table, drinking and laughing. He purposefully walks away.

MEMOIR SUBPLOT #2: Al is attracted to his next-door neighbor, Sheila.

- **Approximately p. 80:** Sheila, Al's neighbor, a divorcée, is chatting with Mary, Al's wife, at the community swimming pool. While they're talking, Sheila's only child, three-year-old Marcus, drowns.
- **Approximately p. 160:** Sheila shows up at Al's school. She's tearful, still reeling about Marcus, and needs a shoulder to cry on. They go for coffee. Al misses taking his dad to a doctor's appointment.
- **Approximately p. 240:** Mary tells Sheila to butt out. Sheila immediately tells Al what Mary said.
- **Approximately p. 320:** Sheila calls Al and asks him to take her to the casino. He says no, then changes his mind, and they go. Knowing his proclivities, Mary tracks him down and catches him and Sheila at a blackjack table. He apologizes and uses some of his winnings to send Sheila home in a limo so he can focus solely on Mary.
- **At the end:** Sheila comes to his school again and invites him for coffee. He declines.

Note how each subplot stands alone—it has a beginning, a middle, and an end. In the thriller, Kayla succeeds in getting her mom to understand her own limitations and to free herself from Bill. That she also won her custody case and is moving to Florida with her kids is not mentioned—those elements are dealt with in the primary plot. Likewise, in the memoir, Al gets his gambling under control and begins to repair his relationship with Mary, his wife. You don't know how the rest of his life is going—those issues are dealt with in the primary plot.

While it might appear that you're considering subplots in isolation from your primary plot, you're not. Think of yourself as a weaver, intertwining plot threads of varying thicknesses and colors. Ultimately, the design resolves itself into one unified piece.

USE THEMATIC AND RECURRING SUBPLOTS IN SERIES

When you write a series, think of each book as a stand-alone novel that features the same cast of characters. Your subplots should follow this same pattern. They should be thematic and recurring, so you carry your high-concept idea from one novel to the next. The subplots stay the same; the incidents that illuminate them change. Here are some examples:

- Robert B. Parker's Spenser books, which can be viewed as cozies for men, feature a self-reliant private eye named Spenser. In every novel where Spenser's love interest, Susan, appears, a subplot involves the sanctity of romantic love. (Susan first appears in *God Save the Child*, the second book in the series.) Each book also features a subplot about the link between honor and self-esteem, as well.
- John D. MacDonald's Travis McGee novels feature an idealized amateur detective, a "salvage consultant," who'll help you salvage what he can, for a share of the booty. Travis is a free spirit, yet loyal and self-reliant. And sexy. Men want to

be him. Women want to be loved by him. Each of the books includes two subplots: one about isolation and loneliness (often involving an important secondary character, the brilliant, but depressed, economist Meyer); the other, the emotional value of revenge.

- My Josie Prescott mysteries always feature an antiques-themed subplot (in addition to the primary antiques plot) and a romantic interlude between Josie and her boyfriend, Ty.
- Brian Thiem's police procedurals feature an Oakland police homicide sergeant, Matt Sinclair, who hunts the city's most dangerous killers. The first two in the series are 2015's *Red Line* and 2016's *Thrill Kill*. Each one includes a subplot involving Sinclair's struggles with romance and another about his inability to forgive himself for his turbulent past. Both add robustness to the character, enabling readers to identify with the man behind the shield.
- The Hunger Games trilogy, Suzanne Collins's dystopian novels (published in 2008, 2009, and 2010), include important subplots of teenage love, both star-crossed and triangular. A second subplot focuses on the importance of unity in the struggle to succeed.

FIGURE 5.3: NAVIGATE THE SUBPLOT PROCESS

Now it's your turn. As you answer the questions posed in this figure, realize there is no right approach. Answering yes to questions two, four, five, or seven indicate opportunities to create meaningful subplots. Note for *Consigned to Death*, a subplot wasn't created in response to every yes answer. I selected questions two and seven, adding a secondary antiques subplot and another relating to Josie's unwarranted trust of a minor character who, later in the book, becomes a key suspect.

MASTERING SUSPENSE, STRUCTURE, & PLOT

EXAMPLE: *Consigned to Death*, the first Josie Prescott Antiques Mystery

What is the chief nonfiction element in your story? Antiques.

Will readers want to know more about that nonfiction element? Yes. My readers love learning new things and seeing the antiques appraisal process at work.

Describe your protagonist's emotional condition at the start of the story. Josie is reeling; she's weepy, worried, and lonely.

Will developing a plotline based on your protagonist's emotional condition reveal a secret? No. Josie knows why she's upset and so do the readers.

Does some element of your setting lend itself as a subplot? Yes. The rugged New Hampshire coastline reflects the isolation that Josie feels.

Describe your protagonist's most significant weakness. Josie is gullible but doesn't know that about herself. She trusts easily.

Can that character quirk or flaw be developed into a secondary story line? Yes. Josie could fall for a guy who might have a good line but not be a good man, or she could trust that a suspect's explanation of something is accurate, when it isn't.

Subplots help you create layered stories featuring multifaceted characters. Select them with care and integrate them well. Write your subplots so your readers can't see how they influence the primary plot and/or character transformation until the denouement. That's how you structure your story to build suspense.

Congratulations! Your plotting is done. You know your primary story, where TRDs will occur, and now you've entwined your plotline with tendrils from two subplots. The next step in the writing process is to consider how isolation builds suspense. This complex issue is the subject of chapter six.

CHAPTER SIX

ISOLATE YOUR PROTAGONIST—AND EVERYONE ELSE

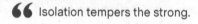

66 Isolation tempers the strong. 99

—PAUL CÉZANNE

ISOLATION, A TOOL OF SUSPENSE

Isolation might temper the strong, but it also can crush the weak. In order to capitalize on this complex tool's multifaceted strengths, you need to understand its power. Both physical isolation (e.g., solitary confinement) and social isolation (e.g., social anxiety leading to agoraphobia) can be used in three ways: as a plot point or TRD, as a theme, or as backstory to explain a certain character attribute. In this chapter, we'll examine all sides of isolation. We'll discuss how to use isolation to drive action and consider how isolation can be used thematically. We'll also examine how isolation can explain certain behaviors and

MASTERING SUSPENSE, STRUCTURE, & PLOT

lead to others, an important component in developing credible characterizations. First, though, let's review the research to understand isolation and its effects.

ISOLATION OVERVIEW

There are two types of isolation: physical and social. Physical isolation occurs when someone is prevented from interacting with other people. Social isolation occurs when people feel as if they don't fit in; when people are shunned, bullied, or otherwise prevented from belonging to a certain group; or when something inside them precludes them from joining in.

Evidence overwhelmingly points to the fact that humans are innately social creatures. Social psychologists report that we want to be wanted. We want to be liked. We want to be part of various groups, ranging from religious organizations to nonprofit organizations, from hunting clubs to book clubs, and from neighborhood parties to political parties. Human beings seem wired to socialize. People who participate in social events live happier and longer lives. Even introverts and recluses, as disinclined to join in as they may be, benefit from social activity.

Thus it is rare that people who endure isolation escape unscathed. Being isolated has been linked to various physical ailments, such as heart disease. It is also closely aligned with depression and anxiety, and is one of the contributing factors often identified in people who attempt or commit suicide. When we are excluded from social interactions, we wither.

Isolation is also an effect or a side effect of certain conditions and situations, such as schizophrenia, autism, anxiety, being shunned, imprisonment, domestic violence, and immigration. Understanding how each kind of isolation can be used to develop or enhance a story will help you to write more believable characters and situations. This, in turn, creates organically heightened tension and suspense.

WHEN ISOLATION IS CENTRAL TO THE PLOT

You can use these research-based facts about isolation as the underlying premise or theme of your stories, or you can use them to add believability to action scenes and enhance a character's credibility. Let's start by looking at examples of how each category of isolation, physical and social, can be used to drive action, reveal character, and build suspense.

You'll recall from chapter three, that one advantage of using Jane's Plotting Road Map is to take your overall story arc and break it into manageable chunks so you can write from one plot point to the next, thus making the writing process easier to navigate. Whether you've already completed your plotting road map or are still in the thinking stage of plotting, it's never too late or too early to add the element of isolation. Your entire story can focus on finding community, or you can add a dollop of isolation to increase tension to a specific scene. Simply interjecting one or more aspects of isolation into a character's backstory or into a situation increases suspense.

For instance, you'll recall from Case Study #1, the domestic thriller (see Figure 3.4), that Kayla asks the police to walk through her house after her purse is stolen—after all, the thief has her driver's license, so he knows where she lives:

> The police drive Kayla home and conduct a walk-through to confirm no one is inside. She locks every door and window. She reaches for the phone to call her unloved sister, her only nearby family, when she hears her cell phone's distinctive ringtone sounding from somewhere inside the house—the cell phone that had been in her stolen purse.

My next plot point has her calling the police from her neighbor's house. In order to write this transition, I need to assess the dozens of options I could use to get Kayla from her house to her neighbor's. Should I have Kayla run for her life screaming like she's crazed? Should I have her back up slowly, holding her breath, until she runs into the wall? Should I have her freeze, paralyzed with fear? As I decide how to get Kayla from her own kitchen to her neighbor's door, one aspect I should weigh is how isolation factors into my choices.

The situation is already rife with tension. The more I can isolate Kayla, the more palpable the tension, and the more vivid the scene, the more suspenseful it becomes. Here's what I have going for me, isolation-wise, based simply on facts that have already been revealed.

- Kayla is alone in her house when she hears her stolen cell phone ring—or she thinks she is alone.
- The responding police officers have left her on her own; as far as they're concerned, it's now up to the detectives to follow up on the purse snatching and car theft.
- The police have no reason to suspect violence.
- The police have no reason to think Kayla was specifically targeted. On the face of it, the theft seems like a crime of opportunity.
- The only person Kayla could think to call is her "unloved sister."
- When Kayla locked the doors and windows, she thought she was keeping the bad guys out—now she realizes she's locked herself in.

The reader doesn't yet know anything about Kayla's relationship with her ex-husband or why she lost custody of their children beyond the mere facts of the situation—we're only on page 15. Maybe, to add a thematic element, I should reveal the divorce was nasty and that she voluntarily gave up custody of her kids because she's fighting depression. After all, the divorce was her choice. Even though Kayla is the one who wanted out of the marriage, she still harbors resentment since the man she thought was her knight in shining armor couldn't save her from devastating depression. Her panic at hearing her cell phone ring is irrationally laced with anger—it's all her ex-husband's fault. If he were a better man, she wouldn't be single again and utterly alone. Thinking of ways to add isolation to an already fraught situation has added richness and complexity to Kayla's character.

Honing in on Kayla's physical and emotional isolation makes my writing task easier—I know I want to capitalize on every aspect of isolation I possibly can. Each sentence will snap with the reality of Kayla's aloneness and vulnerability or foreshadow its consequences. Suspense will build naturally since it's intrinsic to the situation and the character.

PHYSICAL ISOLATION: YOU'RE ALL ALONE

Think of all the ways you could end up utterly alone. Whatever the specific scenario, imagine how it feels. Some people are terrified. Others become enraged. Some rise to the occasion and escape, cope, or strategize. Others freeze or panic. Some people have heart attacks and die. Others weep, overwhelmed with grief or self-pity. Figure 6.1 lists a variety of situations that result in physical isolation. Note that the examples cover a range of genres from literary nonfiction to literary fiction, from memoir to children's literature. Physical isolation is powerful, no matter the genre.

FIGURE 6.1: PHYSICAL ISOLATION PLOTS AND THEMES

SCENARIO: Lost in a mountain wilderness

EXAMPLE: *Lost on a Mountain in Maine* by Donn Fendler as told to Joseph B. Egan, 1978, true adventure/memoir

SCENARIO: Cut off from civilization on a deserted island

EXAMPLE: *Robinson Crusoe* by Daniel Defoe, 1719, literary fiction

SCENARIO: Set adrift on a raft in shark-infested waters

EXAMPLE: *Unbroken: A World War II Story of Survival, Resilience, and Redemption* by Laura Hillenbrand, 2010, literary nonfiction

SCENARIO: Locked in a garret

EXAMPLE: *Jane Eyre* by Charlotte Brontë, 1847, literary fiction

SCENARIO: Cast into a rat-infested dungeon

EXAMPLE: *The Tale of Despereaux: Being the Story of a Mouse, a Princess, Some Soup and a Spool of Thread* by Kate DiCamillo, 2004, children's literature (third grade up)

SCENARIO: Sentenced to solitary confinement

EXAMPLE: *Solitary* by Alexander Gordon Smith, 2011, middle school novel (eighth grade up)

SCENARIO: Condemned to live (and die) in a padded, windowless room where there is no light, where you never see anyone, and where no one ever talks to you

EXAMPLE: *Princess: A True Story of Life Behind the Veil in Saudi Arabia* by Jean Sasson, 1992, literary nonfiction/memoir

SOCIAL ISOLATION: YOU FEEL ALL ALONE

Some of the most poignant and gripping stories revolve around social isolation. The research is clear. Without tangible connections to loving people, infants fail to thrive. Sometimes they even die. Sometimes they become serial killers. A notable pattern among serial killers is they were isolated from their peers when they were children. Some were fat kids, teased and bullied. Others suffered from learning disabilities or they were klutzy or they started at the school midsemester. Something happened to these children—maybe a lack of caressing when they were babes in arms—and they never learned how to create rapport, handle criticism, or empathize. Social isolation grips characters like a vise. Entire books can revolve around issues that derive from social isolation.

Figure 6.2 describes situations in which people find themselves outside the social mainstream. How they deal with the social isolation is the subject of the book. Note how this theme transcends genre; examples range from romance to literary fiction to memoir to middle school novels.

FIGURE 6.2: SOCIAL ISOLATION PLOTS AND THEMES

SCENARIO: The existential anxiety of a frustrated and bored suburban housewife

EXAMPLE: *Diary of a Mad Housewife* by Sue Kaufman, 1967, women's fiction

SCENARIO: A young teen's depression following an acquaintance rape and the ostracism that followed

EXAMPLE: *Speak* by Laurie Halse Anderson, 1997, middle school novel

SCENARIO: Undiagnosed clinical depression

EXAMPLE: *The Bell Jar* by Sylvia Plath, 1963 (first published under the pseudonym Victoria Lucas), literary fiction, generally considered to be a roman à clef (a work of fiction based on fact)

SCENARIO: A runaway bride, shunned by the Amish community

EXAMPLE: *The Shunning* by Beverly Lewis, 1997, romance

SCENARIO: A jazz pianist loses two fingers and shuts himself off from the music scene he loves.

MASTERING SUSPENSE, STRUCTURE, & PLOT

ISOLATION DRIVES CHARACTERIZATIONS

You'll recall from Case Study #2, the memoir, that Al's teenage son, Stewart, has been arrested—again. We don't know why. Knowing we want to highlight elements of isolation, let's create a backstory that illuminates Stewart's private nightmare as he floats in a sea of apparent suburban normalcy.

Al's wife, Mary, was raped—and she got pregnant. Deeply religious and vehemently opposed to abortion, she decided to bear the child. Mary planned to give the baby up for adoption, but her judgmental mother guilted her into keeping it. Mary did what she believed to be the right thing, the moral thing: She kept the baby. She didn't know she'd be unable to love the child. She always made certain Stewart had clean clothes to wear and healthy food to eat, but she could never bring herself to hug him or cuddle him or read to him. In fact, whenever she looked at him, images of the rape flooded her brain. By the time he was six months old, she loathed him. Al had his own issues, too: resentment that Mary decided to keep the baby, shame at his resentment, and guilt that he too can't love Stewart. While Mary froze Stewart out with silence, Al overcompensated, acting the part of loving father, confident in his belief that his secret was secure. Stewart doesn't know he is a rapist's child. He doesn't know why his parents don't love him; he just knows they don't. This scenario is fraught with isolation, from dark despair to pale pretense.

Now that I know Al and Mary's secrets, the essence of their aloneness, every line I write will convey a gravitas that simply wouldn't be possible had I not delved into their backstory, if I hadn't worked to understand the nature and origin of their social isolation. Al thought his memoir would be more anecdotal. Instead it ended up more thematic. It's important to note I won't reveal the backstory through exposition; rather, I'll use incidents to show how isolation manifests itself to these people at this time and in this place.

FAQ

Q: I'm writing a family saga and one of the characters, an eccentric scientist, is a loner. He grew up in a loving home. There was no isolation, per se. He was simply a bookworm. Do I need to add elements of isolation anyway?

A: I think your point is well taken. My brother Mike was an electrical engineer. I recall going to a family party when I was about seven and Mike was about seventeen. He sat in a corner reading the current issue of *Scientific American*. Occasionally people would drift over and he'd chat happily with them for a while. Then they'd drift away and he'd pick up his magazine again. He never sought anyone out, but he was receptive when approached. On the drive home Mike couldn't stop talking about what a great party it was. I remember being amused at the time, and I still smile recalling the incident. Bookworms self-isolate, so there is already a kind of social tension inherent in your character's makeup. If I were writing a character based on my brother, for instance, I'd focus on the paradox—Mike was a loner who loved people.

I might write a scene in which Al is in the kitchen loading the dishwasher after dinner. He's alone. Mary has already gone to bed with her current book, a romance. Stewart and a friend, another outcast named Tom, are sitting on the back porch talking about girls. Al overhears Tom talk about a girl in his English class named Andi, saying he'd never noticed her in particular until the teacher called on her to read the opening vignette from *Sold* (Patricia McCormick's 2006 novel, *Sold*, was a finalist for the National Book Award.)

> Stewart chortled. "I didn't know girls could read out loud," he said.
>
> Tom talks more about Andi, totally unaware of the dagger-like comment Stewart just hurled at his mom. Stewart's mother never read to him when he was young, and that fact has colored his view of women. Al, listening in, got Stewart's sarcastic swipe at his mother, and wishing he were a better man, another kind of man, he finishes the dishes and heads upstairs to bed.

ISOLATION CAN BE HIDDEN IN PLAIN SIGHT

Consider the haunting stories you could write based on these quotes about isolation and loneliness:

- "A prisoner is a man buried alive." (Charles Dickens, after visiting a Pennsylvania prison)
- "Being a prime minister is a lonely job … you cannot lead from the crowd." (Margaret Thatcher, former prime minister of Great Britain)
- "A splendid desert—a domed and steepled solitude, where the stranger is lonely in the midst of a million of his race." (Mark Twain, describing New York City)
- "I was very depressed when I was nineteen. I would go back to my apartment every day and I would just sit there. It was quiet and it was lonely. It was still. It was just my piano and myself. I had a television and I would leave it on all the time just to feel like somebody was hanging out with me." (Lady Gaga, best-selling pop singer)
- "The mass of men lead lives of quiet desperation." (Henry David Thoreau, author, naturalist, abolitionist, and philosopher)
- "Who knows what true loneliness is—not the conventional word but the naked terror? To the lonely themselves it wears a mask. The most miserable outcast hugs some memory or some illusion." (Joseph Conrad, author)

- "It is strange to be known so universally and yet to be so lonely." (Albert Einstein, theoretical physicist)
- "As far as I knew, white women were never lonely, except in books. White men adored them. Black men desired them and black women worked for them." (Maya Angelou, author)

If you look at the lives of these luminaries, it's odd to think they could possibly feel isolated. The lesson here is we can never know what secrets hide in the hearts of our neighbors or relatives or friends—often we barely know the truth about ourselves.

This tendency we humans share to present a happy face to the world reflects another way of thinking about isolation. When we let people see only one side of us, we are, by definition, isolating ourselves. Yet, if telling the truth opens you up to ridicule or attack, why would you reveal your fears or shames or secrets? Why would your characters?

As an author, you can use this shared human trait to develop believable scenes of action, a theme that resonates, and characters your readers will find empathetic.

WRITING EMOTIONAL TRUTH

Whether the isolation you're writing about is literal, like Lee Child's epic hero, Jack Reacher, who has no home and travels only with a toothbrush; or metaphorical, like the rugged, lonely coast of my protagonist Josie Prescott's adopted home, New Hampshire, the same precepts about showing, not telling—a hallmark of all strong writing—apply. Find the words to make the emotion evident. As Anton Chekov explained, "Don't tell me the moon is shining; show me the glint of light on broken glass." When you hone in on emotional truth, your stories take on a greater importance than if you skirt emotionally resonant issues. Find fresh ways to showcase truths about the human condition—because readers long to understand themselves and others.

METAPHORS ILLUMINATE ISOLATION

The more specific your descriptions of how isolation feels, the more memorable your underlying message will be. To help intangible ideas and emotions become real, you might consider creating metaphors.

As you no doubt know, a simile is a figure of speech used to compare two apparently unrelated things using the words *like* or *as*. For example, this sentence is a simile: "When my husband hugs me, it's like I've reached a safe harbor." A metaphor is a figure of speech comparing two apparently unrelated things *without* using the words *like* or *as*. That same concept written as a metaphor might read: "I reached the safe harbor of my husband's arms." Extended metaphors dig deeper into allusion to highlight the comparison or to accentuate one element of it. In the 2010 memoir, *Fixing Freddie: A TRUE story about a Boy, a Single Mom, and the Very Bad Beagle Who Saved Them*, Paula Munier uses the metaphor of atmospheric pressure that builds until it bursts into a storm to describe her isolation and loneliness.

> I didn't cry for Isis then, or in the hot summer days that followed. I worked, and I came home to the cottage. I fed the dogs, and walked them through the bogs. I watched stupid sitcoms and sappy movies and sat down by the water with Shakespeare and Freddie under the stars, drinking red wine and feeling sorry for myself. But I, the champion crier, did not cry.
>
> Weeks later, not long before Mikey was due home, a big storm hit the South Shore. The wind tore around the little cottage; torrents of rain pounded the roof. Choppy waves formed whitecaps on the lake. I stood out on the screened porch with the dogs, only somewhat protected from the driving rain. Lightning flashed, brightening the great pond. Thunder boomed, and the dogs thundered in return.
>
> The tempest raged all around me. Sheets of rain pelted the porch, penetrating the screens and smattering me with warm gushes of wet

mist. The tears, too, came in a rush. While Freddie and Shakespeare howled along with the wind, I cried for the dear cat who'd brightened our lives for eleven years. I cried for Mikey, stuck at Miss Priss's house for yet another summer. And I cried for myself, alone on a hot stormy August night on the pond, with no one for company but two increasingly badly behaved dogs.

Similarly, in her 2012 thriller, *Nightwatcher*, *New York Times* best-selling author Wendy Corsi Staub reveals a couple's emotional truth through the well-known "empty nest" metaphor. The term "empty nester" is trite, but there's nothing ho-hum about Corsi Staub's handling of the complexity underlying the cliché. It is fresh and insightful, and does more than merely convert abstract ideas and emotions into something you can see, touch, and measure—it allows readers the pleasure of discovery.

> Vic shifts his gaze to the framed photos on his desk. One is of him and Kitty on their twenty-fifth wedding anniversary last year; the other, more recent, shows Vic with all four of the kids at the high school graduation last June of his twin daughters.
>
> The girls left for college a few weeks ago. He and Kitty are empty-nesters now— well, Kitty pretty much rules the roost, as she likes to say, since Vic is gone so often. "So which is it—a nest or a roost?" he asked her the other day, to which she dryly replied, "Neither. It's a coop, and you've been trying to fly it for years, but you just keep right on finding your way back, don't you?"
>
> She was teasing, of course. No one supports Vic's career as wholeheartedly as Kitty does, no matter how many nights it's taken him away from home over the years. It was her idea in the first place that he put aside his planned career as a psychiatrist in favor of the FBI.

Creating unique metaphors is hard, yet when they're done well, they can help raise your writing from the ordinary to the sublime. To help you master this crucial skill, I've designed the Metaphor Machine. It consists of five steps which, taken together, will help facilitate the crystallization process:

MASTERING SUSPENSE, STRUCTURE, & PLOT

1. Sum up the abstract idea or emotion you want to express as a metaphor in one phrase (e.g., we all die, and we all die alone).
2. Write it down along with a reference to one of the five senses (discussed in chapter four) and the word *like* (e.g., the prospect of dying looks like, the prospect of dying tastes like, etc.).
3. Complete the sentences, allowing your imagination free rein.
4. Seek out patterns among your answers to determine a theme.
5. Write it up.

A dying man may be surrounded by people who love him and whom he loves, but "at that moment of last parting," as George Eliot wrote in her 1859 novel, *Adam Bede*, he is alone. Figure 6.3 shows how the Metaphor Machine can help transform this abstract concept—we die alone—into a meaningful description certain to resonate with your readers. To demonstrate the process, let's look at one issue from two perspectives. The first perspective reflects the experience of someone who is not ready to die: a young woman with an untreatable, terminal disease. The second reflects the experience of someone who is ready to die: an old man who doesn't want to live without his wife, who died a month earlier.

You'll note that the figure below poses a series of questions. This approach is a brainstorming technique (step three in the Metaphor Machine process). One note: Don't ever feel as if you're on a hunt for the one right answer. There are countless right answers.

The best strategy is to put yourself in your character's shoes and come up with as many ideas as you can. You'll have an opportunity to assess your work in step four. As you brainstorm options, try hard to separate the creative process from the critiquing process. Judging your work while you're trying to come up with new ideas is a surefire way to sabotage yourself.

Think of it this way: Step three asks for quantity; step four winnows your options as you search for quality.

FIGURE 6.3: THE METAPHOR MACHINE IN ACTION

PERSPECTIVE ONE: A YOUNG WOMAN WHO IS NOT READY TO DIE
To that character, the prospect of dying feels like:

- Standing naked in a burned-out forest in a bitter wind
- Having an itch you can't reach to scratch

To that character, the prospect of dying smells like:

- Garbage left on the curb on a hot summer day
- A musty house

To that character, the prospect of dying tastes like:

- Burned lamb chops
- Sucking on a rotten lemon

To that character, the prospect of dying looks like:

- The black stubs of trees after fire has decimated the forest
- What you would see when you peer out over a precipice on a cloudy night

To that character, the prospect of dying sounds like:

- A siren fading away
- A child wailing

PERSPECTIVE TWO: AN OLD MAN WHO IS READY TO DIE
To that character, the prospect of dying feels like:

- Taking off too-tight shoes
- Running through soft grass on a sunny day after weeks of rain and mud

To that character, the prospect of dying smells like:

- Clean cotton sheets hung out to dry on a sunny day
- A fresh-picked tomato

MASTERING SUSPENSE, STRUCTURE, & PLOT

> To that character, the prospect of dying tastes like:
>
> - A vanilla ice cream cone on a hot summer day
> - Hot chocolate on a cold winter day
>
> To that character, the prospect of dying looks like:
>
> - A meadow filled with wildflowers on a sunny spring afternoon
> - A sunset over the ocean
>
> To that character, the prospect of dying sounds like:
>
> - Like wind chimes tinkling in the night
> - A 250-voice choir singing the Hallelujah Chorus

In Figure 6.3, you'll note there are two examples for each of the five sensual prompts. You should come up with as many as you can. Some people like to work to a timer. For instance, allot thirty seconds for each sensory prompt and see what you come up with. Other people prefer to take their time, delving into the picture, letting themselves feel or see or hear the thing in their mind's eye. Experiment with the process to customize it for your own use.

Once you've completed the brainstorming process (step three), it's time to move to step four, seeking patterns. Consider the first perspective, where three of the five responses include a reference to burnt things. In the second perspective, you'll note answers referencing sunny days.

The last step is to draft some sentences incorporating these images. In this sample sentence, note how the burnt imagery from the first perspective comes together with a reference to emptiness:

> With her last breath, she slipped into the burnt-out forest of a life laid waste, sinking into an abyss filled only with ash and char.

Another author with a different voice might write:

> Crunch, crunch. Dead wood crumbling underfoot. She walked alone through the char into the endless night. Crunch, crunch.

From the second perspective, an author might write:

> He turned his face to the sun and smiled. It was a good day to die.

Using the same imagery, another author might write:

> He ran through the meadow, not really, not today, but the meadow beckoned him in his dreams, and he answered the call.

Or, if the allusion to too-tight shoes attracts you more than sunny days, you might write:

> With his last shallow breath, he felt the same relief he'd felt that day long ago when after a long, lonely day walking the factory floor, he'd finally removed his too-tight shoes.

Now use the Metaphor Machine below to help you express intangible ideas and emotions, like isolation. The more specific the image, the more real it will feel to your readers, and the more real it feels, the more your readers will be engaged with your imagery and your message.

FIGURE 6.4: THE METAPHOR MACHINE

Summarize your scenario by describing a specific abstraction and character you want to work with. Then, come up with one or more specific images that complete the thought expressed in the first answer. When you are finished, seek out patterns among your answers to determine a theme.

- To that character, the [insert abstraction] feels like ...
- To that character, the [insert abstraction] smells like ...
- To that character, the [insert abstraction] tastes like ...
- To that character, the [insert abstraction] looks like ...
- To that character, the [insert abstraction] sounds like ...

No matter your genre or your story line, isolating a character or having a character deal with the consequences of isolation will help you heighten tension, the foundation of suspense. A history of isolation can explain aberrant behavior in those with malevolent intentions, just as isolating your protagonist in real time can test a heroic character's mettle. Using this capability helps you harness the power of suspense.

In chapter seven we're going to continue delving into characterization as a strategy to structure your story and create believable plots. We'll see how you can use people's inclination to believe what they see to develop compelling, suspenseful, and surprising plots.

CHAPTER SEVEN

THE DEVIL MADE ME DO IT

> 66 Human nature is not black and white but black and grey. 99
> —GRAHAM GREENE

UNDERSTANDING HUMAN NATURE

One way to think about human nature is to consider the role of red herrings in controlling reader perceptions. While red herrings are commonly associated with crime fiction, authors of all genres can implement them. Memoirs, literary fiction, and literary nonfiction benefit, too, because red herrings add layers of complexity to plots and characterizations.

Crime fiction writers use red herrings to paint the innocent with the colors of guilt. It's a sobering responsibility. We authors wield awesome power. The words we choose can convince readers that someone who's innocent is, in fact, guilty, and can allow the guilty to go free. How we wield that power dictates how our stories will be perceived—as fair-play puzzles or devil-inspired tales of betrayal.

THE ORIGIN OF THE TERM *RED HERRINGS*

The story goes that in the eighteenth and nineteenth centuries, dog trainers developed a new technique to train their tracking hounds. After the formal training period, the hounds were given one last test: Could the dogs follow the underlying scent if a red herring—a smoked fish—was dragged across the path in an attempt to distract them? If the hound was able to follow the underlying scent, he was good to go. If, however, he followed the scent of the red herring, he needed more training. Recently, the Oxford English Dictionary updated its entry, and suggested the term was first used by journalist William Cobbett in an 1807 article for England's *Weekly Political Register*. Cobbett included an anecdote describing how, when he was a boy, he used a red herring to distract hounds from their tracking responsibilities. The apparently fictional account was intended to illuminate what was, to Cobbett, the press's dereliction of duty. Instead of tracking the government's progress in addressing vital domestic issues, it allowed itself to be distracted by the news that England had vanquished Napoleon. Whatever the origin of the term, writers use red herrings to create false trails through misdirection. It's a narrative element that distracts the reader from an underlying truth, adding suspense and intrigue to your stories.

Red herrings can be structural or visual; they can be tiny details or sweeping observations; they can even be introduced via subtext. There are three broad categories of red herrings that can be used to create those false trails:

- **HUMAN NATURE:** what people think and do
- **DETAILS:** what's included or left out in a description
- **EXPERTISE:** what people know or don't

CAPITALIZING ON HUMAN NATURE

People are odd and idiosyncratic creatures. But we're odd and idiosyncratic in predictable ways, and you can use that predictability to distract and baffle your readers. As we consider the first broad category of red herrings—human nature—note the multitude of options you can adapt for your own use.

STRUCTURAL RED HERRINGS

In Irwin Shaw's *Nightwork* (also discussed in chapter three), the key narrative question seems to be whether the thief will be caught. In actuality, Shaw uses the theft and subsequent investigation as a device that allows the story to follow the thief around the world. We watch as he uses the stolen money to fix his eyes, buy nice clothes, and travel to glamorous resorts where he meets people who expand his horizons, and ultimately, who value him for the man he has become. The larger story arc is not about recovering the stolen money; it's about the transcendent power of reinventing yourself. The stolen money is a structural red herring. It works because of Shaw's knowledge of people— we relish an underdog-becomes-a-top-dog story, we believe in second chances, and we love a good chase.

CONFOUNDING READERS WITH APPEARANCE MISCUES

Sometimes the idea "looks can be deceiving" is all it takes to integrate a believable red herring. Let's say you're writing a novel where a group of friends rent a remote mountain lodge for a weekend. Within the first chapter or two, readers learn there's a serial killer on the loose. They also learn there's a caretaker on the grounds, yet none of the friends have seen him. The first night, as a thunderstorm rages overhead, the friends are in the kitchen preparing dinner. All at once, as thunder booms and lighting flashes, the cellar door bursts open and a grim-looking man with the build of a heavyweight boxer steps into the room. The lights flicker, then go out. Under the strobe-like illumination from the bolts of lightening, the man seems sinister, a deviant—he is an obvious suspect. But he isn't the murderer—he's the caretaker who was up the night before finishing an emergency repair to the boiler. After awakening from a catchup nap at his nearby cottage, he threw on some clothes, and without even bothering to brush his hair, went back to check on the boiler, entering through the outside Bilco doors. He came upstairs to introduce himself to the guests. The caretaker is a red herring—and readers fall for it simply based on his appearance and demeanor.

THE BANDWAGON FALLACY

A useful type of red herring based on human nature is the bandwagon fallacy. The bandwagon fallacy is a form of flawed logical thinking. It occurs whenever one argues for an idea based upon an irrelevant appeal to its popularity.

Let's say you're writing a novel of romantic suspense. One of your characters, Violet, is an envious person. She's not-so-secretly pleased at a glitch she's sniffed out in Mary and Tom's relationship. When Tom doesn't attend Mary's family's party— a party he was invited to and RSVP'd for—Violet slyly whispers to an acquaintance that Mary has always been a little stuck up and now look where it's got her. Mary, she says, got what she deserved. Soon all the girls in the neighborhood have jumped on this bandwagon and are telling all the other girls in the neighborhood the same story. It becomes the popular version of events. In the current lexicon, it's an urban myth. However, its popularity is unrelated to its correctness—it's a bandwagon fallacy—and, possibly, a red herring you can use to your advantage.

THREE COMMON FALLACIES YOU CAN USE

The bandwagon fallacy isn't the only flaw in logic you can use to create suspense. Here are three others you can put to work.

AD HOMINEM: Latin for "to the man." When you attack the person instead of the person's argument, you hope to undermine his or her case without ever arguing against it. Ad hominem attacks can take the form of open confrontation or a subtler casting of doubt on an opponent's character and credibility. In a political thriller, you could have one of the candidates, Wendy, make a calm and rational case for revamping the tax code to eliminate loopholes. Her opponent, Mitch, snickers, then asks the audience, "Can you really believe anything from a woman who doesn't have any children? What does she know about making ends meet?" You'll note Mitch's rhetorical questions make no fact-based claim against Wendy's tax proposal. Depending on how I write it, I can distract my readers from considering the proposal on its own merits and convince them Wendy shouldn't be running at all.

APPEAL TO IGNORANCE: This fallacy uses ignorance as proof of one side or another of an argument. For instance, we have no evidence little green men from Mars have infiltrated our government; therefore, that means they do not exist. Ignorance about something says nothing about its existence or nonexistence. Just because we don't have proof little green men from Mars have infiltrated our government, doesn't mean they haven't.

NON SEQUITUR: Implying that seemingly unrelated facts describe a cause-and-effect relationship can be persuasive even though there is, in fact, no causal relationship. For instance, the incidence of rape goes up in the summer. So do sales of ice cream cones. Yet no one would think that ice cream cone sales cause rape.

THE HALO AND DEVIL EFFECTS

We human beings tend to extrapolate. If a man is kind to animals, we assume he's good through and through—this propensity is called the halo effect. Likewise, if a woman is sarcastic, sniping at everyone for no apparent reason, we assume she's bad through and through—the devil effect. Understanding these proclivities allows you to create unreliable (yet credible) narrators, perplexing (yet logical) situations, and complicated (yet believable) characters. Perception trumps reality every day of the week.

For instance, if you read about a woman who volunteers at a senior center, most people will assume she's also competent, smart, and friendly. By introducing her in an early chapter as a dedicated volunteer, no one will suspect her as the killer—or think that someone so fine could possibly be having an affair with a married man. Or be a thief. She's enveloped by the halo effect.

Similarly, if you write about an employee who's perpetually late, readers are likely to assume that he has other negative work traits, as well. He's probably incompetent, has sloppy work habits, or is lazy. It's the devil effect at work. Later, when we learn the employee is caring for a disabled child and can't leave for work until the day nurse arrives, our perception shifts. We now think this man is heroic, he can do no harm, and we anoint him with a halo. Won't we be surprised to learn he really is the killer?

Think about how you might use these tactics in a novel. You could create a cast of characters, all of whom share a positive view of someone—let's call him Johnny. Johnny is a new employee and word spreads that he's an up-and-comer, a real go-getter. (Note the bandwagon fallacy.)

Johnny believes his own mythology and begins acting more confidently. His confidence inspires other people to help him. As a result of their help and support, Johnny succeeds. His coworkers find it easy to dismiss qualities that don't fit their vision of him. They ignore his sarcasm, for instance, and don't notice, or choose to ignore, how it gets pretty biting sometimes. They make excuses for his occasional surliness, explaining to one another that he's having a hard day, no surprise with the workload he's taken on. In other words, Johnny has a dark side and no one will acknowledge it. I could have Johnny do something dastardly, and some of his co-workers, maybe most of them, if I write it well enough, simply wouldn't believe it.

Human nature—it'll get ya every time.

FAQ

Q: I'm writing a memoir recounting my relationship with my father, who was, it turns out, a bigamist. He was a medical equipment sales rep, so he traveled extensively. After he died, we learned from papers in his safety deposit box that he had a second family in another state. I like the idea of describing him as I knew him—loving, jovial, and attentive—then later, revealing all was not what it seemed. What tips do you have so the revelation doesn't come off as overdramatized for effect?

A: First, the situation is inherently dramatic, so it makes sense that you give it the weight it merits. I wouldn't worry about overemphasis. Second, I would encourage you not to "describe" your dad as loving, jovial, and attentive; instead, write up incidents that allow your readers to see for themselves that he was that kind of man. Taking the show, don't tell approach means readers will see your world through your eyes—and the halo effect will be in full force. When you reveal the truth, again through incident, not exposition, your readers will empathize with the shock and dismay you no doubt felt.

INCORPORATING DETAILS BEFUDDLES READERS

The second broad category of red herrings relates to details you include or leave out. Or—and here's where it gets really delectable—you can have your characters wrongly interpret a known fact or even mention a detail during a casual conversation. Frequently the detail in question is a specific element in a description—a torn hem without an explanation of how it ripped or a red rose in a vase when all the ones in the garden are yellow.

In a historical mystery, you might have a character named Charlotte say the following:

> Oh, Lordie, how does that happen? Wouldn't you think you'd notice when you tear your hem? I think you'd have to because you'd trip, wouldn't you? I know I would! Like that time I was walking with Flora ... well, never mind that ... I bet Anna tore her hem yesterday on those stairs at the Sturley's villa ... did you notice how narrow those steps were? And steep, too. That's an accident waiting to happen, if you ask me.

What the reader doesn't know, because you're choosing not to tell them yet, is Anna tore her hem running away from the squire's unwanted advances; she stumbled on an unseen root in the pathway. As to that red rose, well, the squire gave it to her when she first passed by his garden on her way to the village. After Anna succeeded in breaking free from his embrace, her focus was on fleeing. She didn't realize she'd been clutching the flower her entire way home. Only when she finally reached safety, did she notice she was still holding it, and being a kindhearted girl, she couldn't bear throwing it away, so she stuck it in a vase of yellow roses she'd previously arranged.

Did you notice how Charlotte mentioned her walk with Flora? I bet many of you didn't think anything of it, but I ask you now—why did she bring that up? Was it an irrelevant casual mention? Was it foreshadowing of an important clue to come? Or was it a red herring? What about the torn hem?

The multitude of details under your control is astonishing. You need to include those that matter, that help reveal character or inform your plot. You also need to weave in those details that serve as red herrings and leave out those details that, by their absence, raise a red flag. The latter is an especially effective technique when we're talking about leaving something out that the reader, had they been thinking about it, should have noticed.

In Sir Arthur Conan Doyle's 1892 short story, "Silver Blaze," for instance, Sherlock Holmes solves the crime because a dog *didn't* bark:

> "Is there any point to which you would wish to draw my attention?"
>> "To the curious incident of the dog in the night-time."
>> "The dog did nothing in the night-time."
>> "That was the curious incident," remarked Sherlock Holmes.

To build suspense, you could first plant the detail. A while later, let your readers know a detail is relevant without revealing the specifics. Still later, when the suspense has reached a fevered pitch, you explain. You could, in fact, connect this tactic to a TRD.

Figure 7.1 shows how this technique might be used in Case Study #1, the domestic thriller.

FIGURE 7.1: RED HERRINGS IN CASE STUDY #1

APPROXIMATELY P. 160: Kayla, still fearful, peers out her window at work before dashing to her rental car. A young woman holding a toddler's hand inches along the sidewalk. A middle-aged man wearing an old-fashioned straw Panama hat consults his watch, then looks around as if he's waiting for someone who's late. A man wearing wraparound sunglasses sits in a dark red SUV staring at the front door. Two joggers wearing matching blue jogging suits run by. Marleen, a co-worker, leaves by the side door, runs across the parking lot, and joins the man in the SUV. They kiss. When Kayla glances back, the man in the Panama has vanished. She thinks a car must have pulled up while she was watching Marleen. The woman with the toddler disappears around the corner. The joggers reappear heading back the way they came.

APPROXIMATELY P. 280: Kayla is at the library researching murders in the neighborhood from the 1920s. Since the library hasn't finished converting its microfiche archives to digital files, she's reading newspaper articles sitting at an old microfiche reader. A man wearing a straw Panama catches her eye. Kayla wonders if Panamas are making a comeback.

APPROXIMATELY P. 360: Kayla steps into her house and sees a Panama hat hanging on the newel post.

Is your blood running cold? If you incorporate details as suspense-heightening tools, your readers won't be able to put your book down. Note that I slipped the first reference to the Panama hat into the middle of a list of observations. People tend to remember beginnings and endings better than the mass of information contained in the middle, so that's a smart way to hide the importance of the detail while still playing fair with your readers.

USING A CHARACTER'S EXPERTISE

The final category of red herrings revolves around who knows what, who doesn't, and why. Think of the array of things you don't know. If you're not a gourmand, why would you notice that someone cooked with bottled lemon juice, not fresh squeezed? There's no reason for it to be significant to you unless you have a trained or refined palate. This red herring technique comes up all the time in my Josie Prescott Antiques Mysteries. Josie, an antiques appraiser, notices details that elude laypeople—why wouldn't she? She's an expert in the field.

Let's say someone comes into her shop wanting to sell an antique watch fob. It's gold in color and marked 14 karat. From that one fact Josie will know it's unlikely the fob is an antique— most antique gold is 18 karat, not 14 karat, but the significance of that fact is likely to elude most readers, even if it registers as a bit unusual.

A related red herring is the opposite—trusting an expert who's wrong, such as the family lawyer or a financial advisor.

In Rex Stout's *The Gun With Wings,* Nero Wolfe investigates the apparent suicide of an opera singer. The singer had been recovering from an injury he suffered after getting into a brawl with another man. His larynx was damaged. At first analysis, it seems the singer, feeling hopeless that he'd ever be able to sing again, put a gun in his mouth and pulled the trigger, shooting off the back of his head. But forensic evidence proved otherwise. The killer was his physician, a celebrity doctor who made house calls. He'd messed up the operation and didn't want anyone to discover his malpractice. That's pretty clever plotting, don't you think? Have you ever had a sore throat? Think about that experience—you're worried about your health, you're in pain, your doctor asks you to open wide and say, "ahhh." Who among us wouldn't do just that? There you are with your head back, staring at the ceiling, waiting for the diagnosis. In *The Gun With Wings*, that poor opera singer didn't have a chance. The point is that a doctor has a unique relationship with her patients. In our society, the cultural norm is that doctors are selfless, and to some people, they're godlike heroes. You can capitalize on that belief system to lull your readers into complacency.

This is, of course, the premise behind Agatha Christie's classic, *The Murder of Roger Ackroyd*. The final revelation is considered to be one of the most innovative plot twists in crime fiction. The bottom line is, when dealing with professionals, watch your back.

Think about the trusted professionals in your world. Lawyers. Accountants. Bookkeepers. Bankers. Pharmacists. Who knows your secrets? Whom do you trust?

YOU'RE AN EXPERT ON YOU

It's not only trusted professionals you need to watch out for. If we're talking expertise, you're an expert about yourself and your environment. You rule your own domain.

Imagine a homey experience gone wrong. Kayla (Case Study #1, the domestic thriller), comes home with bags of groceries. She puts them on the counter and begins to place items in cupboards. She's reaching for a door pull when she notices a paring knife from her knife holder is missing. The other knives are there—the six-inch all-purpose blade, the serrated bread knife, even the cleaver. Where's her paring knife? Kayla is already on edge. She looks in the dishwasher. It's not there. She looks in the sink. Nothing. Thinking perhaps she mistakenly slipped it into the flatware drawer, she opens the drawer, knowing she won't find it. She doesn't. Now she's scared for real.

That's the ticket! Your reader's heart will stop.

INTEGRATING RED HERRINGS

Layering clues or red herrings by repeating similar events is a reliable way to build suspense. In this case, perhaps Kayla will find the knife in the refrigerator. She forgot she'd been interrupted by an urgent phone call from her mother while peeling an orange. She'd simply slid the plate containing the half-peeled orange, the peel she'd already removed, and the knife onto the closest shelf in the fridge. When she discovers it, she laughs at herself, maybe joking that she's getting old. Later in the book, maybe Kayla searches for a box cutter to open a box from a mail-order company. It's missing. Kayla finds it on her worktable, but she doesn't recall leaving it there. Toward the end of the book, as Kayla approaches her desk, she sees her cleaver on the blotter.

Can you feel the little hairs on the back of your neck rising?

Is the fact that knives keep disappearing and reappearing innocent foreshadowing? Or are those missing knives red herrings, telling us something about how preoccupied Kayla is?

That one question—is it a red herring or is it at the core of what's going on—summarizes the challenge we authors face in using these artful devices well. They're not a liar's tool—they're a magician's tool. By using red herrings the same way a magician uses sleight of hand, you'll be able to divert your readers' attention from the actual to the illusionary. If done well, your readers will believe what they see on the printed page.

FIGURE 7.2: CHARACTER-DRIVEN RED HERRINGS

The questions listed below are designed to help you think through the process of incorporating red herrings in your stories. As you go through the exercise, take notes about how these tactics can help you build suspense.

- Do any characters enjoy the halo effect? If so, describe the positive attribute(s) your readers admire.
- Do any characters suffer from the devil effect? If so, describe the negative attribute(s) your readers dislike.
- Should a character use a flaw in logic, such as the bandwagon fallacy, to divert readers' attention from a significant issue?
- Is there a detail you can hide in plain sight? What is it? Where will you place it?
- Do any of your characters have special expertise that lets them know things other characters don't? If so, who and what do they know? Be as specific as possible. (Don't simply say a lawyer knows the law; specify he knows the rule against perpetuities.)
- Can you incorporate any of these tactics into your plot by beefing up a TRD? How?

Whether you use red herrings in the conventional sense, to help disguise the killer's identity in a mystery or thriller, or whether you use them in a grander way to add complexity to your plot across genre lines, they must flow organically from your story and characters. They can't be contrived or coincidental. The more subtly intertwined the red herring, the bigger the payoff when the reader ultimately learns the truth.

Speaking of truth, to whatever extent you use red herrings, I encourage you to never lose sight of the importance of protecting innocence. If you've smirched a character's reputation to take your readers' eyes off the killer, you must restore that character's good name. Yes, you need to assign guilt, but you also need to protect innocence. If you do all that, you'll have written a book readers admire and can't put down. Those are the books that get published.

MASTERING SUSPENSE, STRUCTURE, & PLOT

PART TWO

WRITING

CHAPTER EIGHT

ADD SURPRISE— SPARINGLY

> 66 A story to me means a plot where there is some surprise. Because 99
> that is how life is—full of surprises.
>
> —ISAAC BASHEVIS SINGER

THE JACK-IN-THE-BOX EFFECT

In 1962, Alfred Hitchcock and Francois Truffaut discussed their work during a marathon lasting fifty hours over five days. The two great directors and their French/English interpreter barely paused for meals. It was during this conversation that Hitchcock gave his famous surprise versus suspense example—the bomb planted in the café. He used this example to demonstrate that contrary to popular belief, suspense is far more engaging than surprise.

Say you have a scene where two characters are talking in a café, and a bomb suddenly goes off under the table—the audience experiences surprise. Your readers' emotional and physiological reactions are likely to be similar to the heart-stopping adrenaline rush a child feels the first time he opens a jack-in-the-box. Can you remember your first time? If you're like most people, you were startled, and for a few seconds, the experience was all consuming. You didn't think of anything else; you didn't notice anything else. Your entire focus was on processing what had just happened. That's the power of surprise.

Contrast that experience with this one: You witness a man approach a café where two people are drinking coffee while enjoying a pleasant chat. You see the man step behind a column and turn an old-fashioned alarm clock to one o'clock. The clock is taped to a bomb. A clock mounted on a nearby wall informs you it's 12:45. You watch as the clock ticks down the time. It's 12:49. The people keep chatting. It's 12:52. The woman laughs. It's 12:57. They finish their coffee. It's 12:59. How do you feel now? If you're like most people, you're holding your breath, waiting for the explosion—or for a hero to rush in and save the day. This approach, showing the viewer or the reader what's going on, translates into fifteen minutes of suspense; all the immediate explosion bought us was fifteen seconds of surprise.

The difference between the immediate explosion and the one we anticipate is that in the latter example, we were fully informed. While the surprise flared up, catching you unaware, the suspense slowly burned, drawing you in.

TELL THE TRUTH AS YOUR CHARACTERS PERCEIVE IT—OR AS THEY WANT IT TO BE PERCEIVED

Keeping your readers fully informed is a hallmark of crime fiction. Traditional mysteries are generally structured as fair-play puzzles, where the reader is limited to the detective's point of view. In thrillers, both the bad guy's and the good guy's intentions are typically known from the start. Readers are fully informed as they watch the villain pit his wily and nefarious skills against those of the virtuous and clever hero.

A newer trend in crime fiction is the unreliable narrator. From a fair-play point of view, your narrator needs to tell the truth as she sees it. If she is going to lie, it needs to be for some specific reason that will be revealed as the story develops. For instance, I could have a character keep a journal filled with lies. Let's call her Briana. Since the journal is private—Briana doesn't show it to a soul—at first glance, this looks like an unfair interaction with my readers. However, let's say Briana plans on killing her lover. A journal going back months painting a picture of a passionate, devoted relationship between them would be a compelling piece of evidence in a police investigation, and if necessary, for a jury. As the story unfolds, Briana's unreliable narration becomes understandable. In fact, keeping that journal will impress readers with Briana's foresight and diligence; it is, after all, a brilliant Machiavellian move.

Part of the complexity here relates to the multiple meanings of the word *surprise*. Readers don't want surprises that feel fake or forced, or that reveal a lack of continuity. Appropriate surprises are those that might logically happen in life and that organically lead to suspenseful moments.

This begs the question, of course, that if suspense is so much more gripping than surprise, and if the effect is more lasting, why use surprise at all? The answer provides a twofold peek in the writer's toolbox. First, surprise can delight on its own, and second, it is one of the most reliable ways to launch your readers into situations fraught with heightened tension—a cornerstone of suspense. The following excerpt from chapter twelve of *Lethal Treasure*, the eighth book in the Josie Prescott Antiques Mystery series, shows you how adding a dollop of surprise takes a routine exchange in an unexpected direction. As you read, notice how Josie reacts to the surprise and how it changes her feelings about Scott.

"How are you doing?" I asked Scott.

He looked at me over his shoulder. "I've been better. You?"

"Same."

He nodded, then turned back to watch the snow. "Now that's a storm."

I joined him at the window. Wind-swept drifts made it hard to tell for sure, but it looked as if four or five inches had already accumulated. The dark-colored cars parked along the side appeared veiled in white; the white ones were nearly invisible.

"It sure is," I agreed.

"What's the forecast?" he asked. "Do you know?"

"Unpredictable. The weatherman says it depends on upper level winds or something. From an old-timer in the know, I hear two feet."

"Two feet … that's no joke. I can't remember if I've ever been in a storm that dropped two feet of snow."

"Where are you from?"

"New York … the city … we get plenty of snow, but if anything like this happened … I don't know … maybe I was out of town."

"I lived in New York for a few years. It's the buildings, I think, and the subway. Most of the time, they keep the sidewalks and roads warm enough to limit accumulation."

"Plus, in Rocky Point, we're more than three hundred miles farther north."

"That, too." The wind shifted and flakes spun sideways, peppering the window. "Driving isn't going to be any fun tonight."

"Thanks for the warning." He flexed his back muscles. "So much for a quiet country weekend." He shook his head. "How long have you been up here?"

"Nine years, going on ten."

"Quite a difference from New York."

"Yeah … I love it here." I smiled a little. "But I love the city, too. Chocolate and vanilla, both good."

"Leigh Ann's the same. She loves both places." He looked around, then turned back to the window. "They've been talking to her a long time now. Do you know what about?"

"I was with her for awhile, then they wanted to ask her questions privately … personal stuff, I suppose."

He nodded. "They asked me plenty of personal questions, and I never even met the guy."

"Were you able to tell them anything helpful?"

"Who knows? Mostly I said 'I don't know.' I don't know who wanted to kill him. I don't know if they were having money problems. I don't know if their marriage was on the rocks."

"Really?" I asked. "I thought you and Leigh Ann were close. I would have expected her to have confided in you."

His eyes remained on the blowing snow. "Sure, we talk. But you know how that goes. You only know what someone chooses to tell you, right? It can feel like they're confiding in you until you figure out they're towing the party line, not telling you how they really feel." He shrugged. "Case in point: I just told you that Leigh Ann loves it here. Maybe she does. Or maybe she just wanted me to think she loves it here. Pride, you know?"

"Sounds like you guys have some history."

He turned toward me and grinned, a frisky one. "You might say that. We were married for ten years."

"What?" I gawked, then laughed, enjoying a rare moment of genuine surprise. I expected to hear a tale of star-crossed lovers, not that they'd been married. "Well, you just proved your point, didn't you: You never can tell. I had no idea Leigh Ann was married before. When did you guys divorce?"

"About three years ago." He turned back to the window. "I was the stupid one … I fell for a leggy blonde named Natasha, just like in the movies. Whoever said, 'There's no fool like an old fool,' had me in mind, except I wasn't all that old. Thirty-two at the time, to be exact."

"John Heywood. My dad changed it a bit. 'There's no fool like an old fool except a young one.'"

"That's funny. And true. Who's John Heywood?"

"A sixteenth-century playwright who married well. He was employed through four royal courts, which is quite an accomplishment in any circumstances, and downright extraordinary when you think that he was a devout and vocal Catholic and one of the four monarchs he served under was King Henry. I've always wondered why King Henry didn't have him beheaded."

"Maybe he liked his plays and didn't care about his religious beliefs."

"Probably. Did you marry her? The leggy blonde named Natasha?"

"Of course. Didn't I mention I was a fool? The marriage lasted about twenty minutes. Fifteen, really, but we were stuck in traffic leaving the chapel, so I call it twenty."

I laughed. "I'm sorry. I don't mean to laugh at you."

"Feel free. I'm laughing at myself."

"At least you realized you'd made a mistake and fixed it."

"You're kind to say so, but you're off the mark. My foolishness ran far deeper than you know ... I lied to Leigh Ann for two years." His left hand formed a fist and he soft pounded the window frame. "I was embarrassed to admit what a screw-up I'd been so I told her everything was hunky dory. Let's repeat that quote again, this time in unison—I'll take the role of the fatally flawed hero if you play the Greek chorus. 'There's no fool ...'" He shrugged.

"And then, after you found the courage to tell her the truth, you discovered she'd married Henri."

"God loves irony."

"And may be lying to you about how happy she was," I said, thinking aloud. "How did you come to be up here?"

"Leigh Ann thought we could be friends. She told me that I'd like Henri and that he'd like me." He paused for a moment and his expression shifted from self-deprecating to somber. "It's kind of like wiggling a loose tooth with your tongue. You know it's going to hurt like hell, but you do it anyway."

"You still love her."

"When I married Natasha I thought I was in love with her, that Leigh Ann and I had grown apart ... you know, that it was over. I was wrong. Turns out, I just succumbed to momentary lust while in the throes of temporary insanity. Not to sound like a dude out of a romance novel or anything, but my heart belongs to Leigh Ann, always did."

We stood side by side for a few minutes, neither of us talking, both of us watching the snow and thinking private thoughts. I liked Scott. He was funny and outgoing and open. He also had one heck of a motive for murder.

The best surprises add significant insights to the characters involved in that surprise, while setting up future suspenseful situations. As Josie notes in this excerpt from *Lethal Treasure*, the fact that Scott still adores Leigh Ann catapults him into the murder investigation. A person who wasn't on anyone's radar becomes a suspect because of a surprise.

EVERYDAY SURPRISES

As my 83-year-old mother and I inched across the mall parking lot that winter, she confided that she hated walking like an old lady, always on the lookout for black ice, always wearing sensible shoes. She wanted to stride along with the movers and shakers wearing the high heels that showcased her million-dollar legs.

A week later she slipped on a patch of ice and crash-landed on the sidewalk.

That my mother slipped is a surprise. I foreshadowed it a bit, but there was no particular reason for you to see it coming. That unexpected turn of events is a hallmark of surprise and helps differentiate it from suspense. Note also how it differs from twists, reversals, and moments of heightened danger (TRDs are discussed in chapter three).

A twist takes you in a different direction than you expected, which might be a surprise, but is a reflection of a plot development, not a one-off event. A reversal takes you in the opposite direction than you expected, which might also be a surprise, but is also a reflection of plot development, not a one-off event. Moments of heightened danger occur without changing the plot path—the danger might or might not be a surprise.

To keep your readers on the edge of their seats, you need to integrate surprises that lead slowly, inexorably, and with deadly calm, to suspense. In order to do so, you need to understand what makes a surprise effective.

MASTERING SUSPENSE, STRUCTURE, & PLOT

THE ANATOMY OF SURPRISE

There are good surprises, like an unexpected visit from a much-loved distant friend or relative, and bad surprises, like an unexpected cancer diagnosis. Good or bad, all surprises share one key characteristic—they're unforeseen. Integrating surprises into your stories can delight, intrigue, captivate, titillate, move, worry, and/or inspire your readers. The trick is to set them up so they feel fitting, not merely plunked down for effect. You'll notice that I set up my mother's fall by showing (not mentioning) her fear of falling. The surprise felt appropriate because it was logical given the situation.

FAQ

Q: What about surprise endings? Is it all right to have a last-minute surprise, or should you only insert surprises that lead to suspense?

A: Don't mistake a final, startling denouement that includes a surprise for a contrived moment at the end where your readers go "huh?" A surprise is a singular, unexpected event, not a conclusion or a "reveal" laden with coincidence or absurdity. That said, surprise endings are, if done well, ideal. A solution that readers don't see coming, but which, once revealed, feels inevitable, is a true reader-pleaser. Mega-bestsellers *Gone Girl* by Gillian Flynn and *The Girl on the Train* by Paula Hawkins are structured to include a final, fitting, yet unexpected twist.

Another best-selling novel, Jodi Picoult's *My Sister's Keeper*, includes two final twists. Some critics claimed the second was gratuitous and manipulative, but Picoult maintains it was mandatory and appropriate. Regardless of your view of that final denouement, the ending is jaw dropping. One successful approach in crime fiction is to correctly identify the killer, but at the last minute reveal that her motive was wrongly understood. For instance, Salina, known in her community as devoted to her mother, Tia, dreams of traveling the world. Salina takes Tia to church on Sundays and Bingo on Wednesdays. At the end of the mystery, when it's revealed that Salina killed her mother, and that it was not the grafter or the law-

yer or whoever else I've planted as a suspect, everyone assumes
Salina did it for the insurance money. But Salina had been saving for
her around-the-world cruise for a decade. Money wasn't the issue.
Liberation was. Salina killed her mother to be free. She was up to
her neck with Tia's admonitions and instructions and expectations.
Salina couldn't just leave—her strict religious upbringing precluded
that option. Better for Tia to go to heaven to be with Daddy, Salina
decided, just like she always said she wanted. Are you surprised?
It gets you thinking, doesn't it? And that's the goal.

SET UP SURPRISES

To gain optimum benefit, a surprise requires a setup. To ensure surprises feel natural, while still astounding your readers,
think opposites. What can your character do or say that is opposite to what is expected? My mother, you'll recall, preferred
high heels. The opposite is clomping along in sturdy shoes and
slipping anyway.

As you review the examples in Figure 8.1, note how the surprises described for our two case studies serve to add both di-
mension to the characters and intrigue to the plot. In all four
examples, the surprises work because there's a causal relationship—the outcomes flow organically from the surprise.

FIGURE 8.1: SURPRISE: CAUSE AND EFFECT

GENRE: Women's fiction

PREMISE: Anne, a dowdy, reserved sixty-five-year-old protagonist,
dreams of travel but has never had the money to go anywhere. Now
that she's retired, she sets out on an around-the-world journey of
discovery.

ELEMENT OF SURPRISE: She used to be a librarian.

WHAT'S EXPECTED: Anne will spend more time observing than doing.

WHAT'S OPPOSITE: Anne turns into a glamour-puss extrovert.

HOW IT MIGHT WORK: Anne has a one-night stand with a handsome
stranger she meets in an Italian trattoria. When she wakes up the

next morning, he's gone, along with her cash. This mini-crisis sets up the readers' expectations that her adventures will be increasingly dangerous. This uncertainty contributes to suspense.

GENRE: Young adult paranormal

PREMISE: After Tommy, age seventeen, is knocked unconscious by a line drive during a baseball game, he develops the ability to read minds. At first he thinks it's fun, then he realizes that discovering people's secrets carries an awful weight.

ELEMENT OF SURPRISE: Tommy's mother loathes his father.

WHAT'S EXPECTED: Tommy confronts her, demanding an explanation.

WHAT'S OPPOSITE: Tommy consults a soothsayer he found during a Google search and learns to twist his newfound ability to read minds into an ability to change minds.

HOW IT MIGHT WORK: Tommy plants loving thoughts about his dad in his mother's brain, but unbeknownst to him, they're absorbed literally and instantaneously. A thought of "He's the man of my dreams," for instance, results in his mom napping in the middle of a client meeting at her job. Suspense is derived from the readers' wanting to know what else will go wrong, despite Tommy's good intentions, and what he'll do about it.

GENRE: Case Study #1: Domestic thriller

PREMISE: Kayla reaches for a box of cereal in her suburban grocery store. When she turns back to her cart, she discovers that her purse is gone.

ELEMENT OF SURPRISE: Kayla wakes up to find all the plants surrounding her house are dead.

WHAT'S EXPECTED: Kayla freaks out.

WHAT'S OPPOSITE: Kayla gets mad. She brings in a landscaping professional to analyze what happened. He discovers they were poisoned. Kayla has him replace all the noxious dirt, plant new shrubs and flowers, and then secretly installs a nanny cam to catch the perpetrator, in case she strikes again.

HOW IT MIGHT WORK: The nanny cam reveals Kayla's sister pouring a poisonous mixture into the dirt around the new plants. Now Kayla needs to decide what to do with that information. Tough decisions lead to suspenseful moments.

Surprises delight readers, but they must be formulated with care. You need to maintain the integrity of your story and your characters. You also need to ensure you avoid out-of-nowhere situations. You can't write a traditional mystery, for example, then change course and reveal that the killer is an alien, based on the idea that it's a "surprise." Neither can you write a romance with mysterious twins who suddenly appear for the first time two chapters from the end. That's not a surprise; that's cheating.

The principle of keeping readers as informed as possible not only applies to crime fiction, but to all writing, including memoirs, such as the one about my mom.

> The call informing me my mother was en route to the hospital came from a firefighter. My mother fell in front of the firehouse near her Boston apartment. She was bruised and a little banged up, but otherwise fine. Mostly, she was tickled pink to have been ministered to by three handsome firefighters.
>
> "They're all so good looking," she said as I drove her home from the emergency room. "Do you think it's a requirement of the job?"
>
> A week later we delivered thank you cookies.
>
> The next Saturday, she fell again.

THE DIFFERENCE BETWEEN SURPRISE AND SUSPENSE

Once you understand how surprise can lead to suspense, you can masterfully drop in moments of surprise without sacrificing the slow build-up of tension that is suspense. The following are three tried-and-true techniques: a first occurrence of an unexpected event, an anomaly, and the revelation of a previously unknown fact.

A First Occurrence of an Unexpected Event

Consider the famous spontaneous combustion scene in Charles Dickens's *Bleak House*. In chapter thirty-two, a rag and bottle merchant and collector of papers named Krook (irony in his name intended), whose diet seems limited to gin, burns to ash through spontaneous combustion.

The novel's primary plot revolves around a court case, Jarndyce vs. Jarndyce, in which the court must determine which of several wills is the valid one. With so many potential beneficiaries, the consequences of the decision reach far and wide. Krook's demise, while shocking, serves an important role. It allows access to his papers and creates more than one suspenseful moment as characters search through his hoard. When they find a document that relates to the case, the payoff is clear. The surprise, the spontaneous combustion, is effective and appropriate because it leads to a suspenseful search.

An Anomaly

When children see a clown they expect fun surprises, so discovering that the clown in Stephen King's 1986 novel, *It*, is not the benevolent character it appears to be, but the manifestation of evil, is an astounding surprise; it is an anomaly.

The novel is set in a small town in Maine and alternates between two time periods: the late 1950s and the mid 1980s. We learn that It, an apparently bubbly clown named Pennywise, has eaten children, his preferred prey, and adults, too, for hundreds of years. That Pennywise has succeeded in feeding on children for generations and has just awakened from its twenty-seven-year hibernation, creates a sense of impending doom. As Pennywise sets its sights on each new victim, tension ratchets up. What starts as a surprise morphs into suspense.

The Revelation of a Previously Unknown Fact

In *Seconds*, first published in 1963, author David Ely crafts a tale around the theme that the grass is always greener on the other side of the fence. A secret organization known only as the Company offers dissatisfied people an opportunity for a second chance. You can cast off your boring life and live the life you always dreamed of. The Company stages your death, including leaving behind a corpse that looks like you. They give you a fresh identity, complete with evidence of your accomplishments. Through experimental surgery, you're given a new, younger, more attractive look. Life is, on the surface, perfect. Only later, when we learn how they harvest the bodies they need to stage their clients' deaths, do we see what has been going on behind the scenes. This shocking revelation is a complete surprise; then as suspense mounts, surprise turns into dread, a byproduct of suspense.

Figure 8.2 demonstrates how each of these tactics uses surprise to generate suspense.

FIGURE 8.2: USING SURPRISE TO CREATE SUSPENSE

AN UNEXPECTED EVENT

How to Create Surprise: A first occurrence of an unexpected event:

- Finding a knife in the refrigerator
- Seeing an elderly woman fall on an icy sidewalk
- Discovering your husband, who called to tell you that he would be working late, wasn't at work

How to Use Surprise to Create Suspense: Repeating occurrences of that unexpected event:

- Finding a knife in the refrigerator, then a week later, finding a knife in your sock drawer
- Seeing an elderly woman fall on an icy sidewalk, then, a week later, hearing her call from inside her apartment that she's fallen and needs help
- Discovering your husband, who called to tell you that he would be working late wasn't at work, then, after allowing yourself to believe he missed your call because he was in the restroom, discovering him at a bar chatting with a gangsta-looking woman

AN ANOMALY

How to Create Surprise: An Anomaly

- A jazz sax player inexplicably stands in the middle of an intersection playing soulful tunes of love and loss.
- A tornado pops up out of nowhere on a low-humidity sunny afternoon in New York City.
- A kind and gracious woman goes ballistic in the middle of the grocery store.

How to Use Surprise to Create Suspense: An anomaly that reveals a hidden agenda:

- A jazz sax player inexplicably stands in the middle of an intersection playing soulful tunes of love and loss, thus allowing a pair of bank thieves to slip into the crowd and get away.
- A tornado pops up out of nowhere on a low-humidity sunny afternoon in New York City because the team of scientists at a federal agency decided not to warn people. Frustrated by budget cuts, they let this experience serve as a warning.
- A kind and gracious woman goes ballistic in the middle of the grocery store, leading her son to insist she get a full medical workup.

A PREVIOUSLY UNKNOWN FACT

How to Create Surprise: The revelation of a previously unknown fact:

- The man your protagonist thought was her roommate's old friend is actually her ex-husband—the one she married on a whim last year in Vegas.
- After your great-grandmother dies, you find her membership card for the Communist Party.
- A child discovers that Santa Claus is really Uncle Timmy.

How to Use Surprise to Create Suspense: The revelation of a previously unknown fact that leads to a darker implication:

- The man your protagonist thought was her roommate's old friend is actually her ex-husband—the one she married on a whim last year in Vegas—and now he's turned up to blackmail her.
- After your great-grandmother dies, you find her membership card in the Communist Party, and when you investigate, you find she was on the FBI's watch list.
- A child discovers that Santa Claus is really Uncle Timmy, and now that child believes that it's all right to lie.

If you don't use surprise to build suspense, you risk the unexpected event coming across as contrived. When you allow the stunning situation to contribute to a deeper story line, your readers will feel gratified.

ADD DRAMA THROUGH ACTION

When writing about a surprise, you need to let the story do the talking. Avoid creating false urgency with words and phrases like *suddenly, out of nowhere,* and *unexpectedly.* Also, revise to avoid all forms of the verb *to be* (*is, are, was, were, be, being, been*).

The urgent-sounding words represent a way of "telling, not showing," which as you know, slows your readers down and creates distance between them and your story. The verb *to be* reflects a state of existence, nothing more. You can't avoid all usages, nor should you. But you should ask yourself if there is a more active verb that could make your point. Oftentimes, revising the entire sentence to eliminate the passive verb results in a significantly stronger sentence.

Figure 8.3 demonstrates the power of replacing time-oriented words and all forms of the verb *to be* with more active verbs and more action-oriented situations. As you review these examples, keep in mind there is never a single best way to write something. The examples in this chart show you one approach to avoiding the specific words and phrases discussed in this section. Your approach will, inevitably, be different, reflecting your voice and style.

FIGURE 8.3: WRITE SURPRISE FOR MAXIMUM IMPACT

INSTEAD OF: I was watching TV, flipping channels, wishing I had something fun to do. Suddenly, out of nowhere, a shadow appeared.

WRITE: Nothing on TV held my interest. I stared at the screen mindlessly, wishing I had something fun to do. A shadow caught my eye. I gasped and dropped the remote.

INSTEAD OF: Bernie was a friend, so I was shocked when, out of the blue, he told me he had been married for five years.

WRITE: I gawked. "You're what? Married? For five years? Did I hear you right, Bernie?"

INSTEAD OF: Suddenly, Annette was after me. She was a hater, no question about that. I wish I had been nicer to her.

WRITE: Meet Annette, hater to the stars. Well, not the stars, more like the dweebs. Her pig-eyes zoned in on me, and I knew I was in for it.

You'll recall from chapter three that plot twists, reversals, and moments of heightened danger (TRDs) should be integrated carefully so you maintain control of your story's structure and pacing. The same principle applies to surprises. Don't use too many. In my traditional mysteries, for example, I aim to include one surprise per book, and I place it roughly midway. It's one of the best ways to counteract saggy-middle syndrome, where too little happens for too long a time. A surprise provides an immediate pop of energy.

"Can you think of any reason I shouldn't buy a condo in Boynton Beach?" my mother asked.

"Florida?" I asked, my brow furrowing. "You hate Florida."

"I hate ice more. It has two bedrooms, two bathrooms, and a Florida room."

"You're looking online, right?"

"No, I'm here with Miriam, the realtor. She says it's a deal. Twenty-four thousand three hundred."

"You're in Florida?"

"Yeah. What do you think?"

My mouth opened, then closed, then opened again as I tried to gather my thoughts. "I think this is a little impulsive."

"I prefer to think of myself as decisive."

"Let me call Mike and Dan."

"Why?" she asked. "Don't you trust my judgment?"

"You called me, remember? You asked my opinion. My opinion is I should call my brothers and ask their opinions."

Dan thought it was a good idea. He liked it when our unconventional mother did conventional things. Mike had no opinion.

"If she wants to move," Mike said, "she should move. But you should go down there and check it out. If it sounds too good to be true … you know the rest of that cliché."

I caught the next plane.

The condo my mother selected was lovely, part of a large middle-class complex located midway between I-95 and the beach. She found it after a longtime friend of hers bought in the community and sent regular postcards showing palm trees and waterfront restaurants. The monthly condo fee was $83. I was tempted to buy one for myself.

I called Mike to report.

"How much was it again?" he asked after I finished.

"Twenty-four thousand three hundred. I negotiated a reduction in closing costs."

"I live in Palo Alto. Twenty-four thousand dollars wouldn't buy a doorknob."

"I say she should go for it," I said, scanning the parking lot. All the residents were in their seventies or up, and all the women wore pretty sundresses. "If she hates it, she'll move back to Boston, and we'll have a family vacation condo."

"I agree."

I went back inside the realtor's office where my mother sat reading an old issue of *Family Circle* magazine. I reviewed the contract and told her it looked good to me. She signed with a flourish, then handed Miriam her American Express card.

And that's the story of how my mother bought herself a condo on a credit card.

The surprise—my mother, hoping to buy a condo, has flown off to Florida without a word to anyone—reinvigorates the story and leads to gentle suspense. What will her children think of her plan—is she spontaneous and decisive or simply half-cocked? Will they perceive it as an adventure? Or a misstep? The surprise gets your attention; the suspense holds it.

A THREE-STEP PROCESS

This three-step process helps you integrate surprises that delight or astound your readers while building tension and suspense. The three steps are as follows:

1. Come up with a logical surprise.
2. Determine how that surprise can result in suspense.
3. Write it up focusing on action and dialogue, not exposition.

The exercise contained in Figure 8.4 invites you to put this three-step process to work. It also encourages reflection. As you progress, it's important to pause and consider which techniques are working for you and why, and which aren't and why not. The more you learn about your own writing process, the more successful you'll be.

FIGURE 8.4: EXERCISE: WRITE UP A SUSPENSEFUL SURPRISE

SELECT A PROJECT you're working on or one you want to start. Make some notes about key information such as:

- What is the inciting incident?
- What motivates your protagonist to act?
- What obstacles will he face?
- What is your narrative question?
- Describe your setting or settings.
- Identify your overarching theme.

COME UP WITH A LOGICAL SURPRISE. What might be an effective surprise? Remember our working definition: *A surprise is a singular, unexpected event.* Don't forget the three approaches discussed earlier in this chapter:

- A first occurrence of an unexpected event
- An anomaly
- The revelation of a previously unknown fact

DETERMINE HOW THAT SURPRISE CAN RESULT IN SUSPENSE. Jot some notes to help you determine how your surprise will lead to suspenseful situations. Will it affect a character's behavior? Change the direction of the story?

WRITE IT UP focusing on dialogue or action, not exposition. Draft the scene in which the surprise occurs. As you revise your initial draft, use the following as a checklist:

- Did you use any time-oriented words such as *now* or *suddenly*?
- Did you use any form of the verb *to be*?
- Are all of your verbs action-oriented and highly specific?
- Could you replace exposition with dialogue?
- Could you replace exposition with action?

SUMMARIZE AND REFLECT: As you completed this exercise, what worked well for you? Where did you struggle? What did you learn that you'll be able to apply to your writing going forward?

All the surprises and all the suspense in the world don't matter a whit if your readers don't care about your characters. In chapter nine, we'll look at how to structure character revelations so your readers won't be able to put your books down.

CHAPTER NINE

GET INTO YOUR READERS' HEADS

> " Betrayal is the only truth that sticks. "
>
> —ARTHUR MILLER

STABILITY VS. CONFUSION AND BETRAYAL

Most people long for stability. In fact, safety (sometimes expressed as security) places second on Abraham Maslow's famous hierarchy of needs, just after physiology. Think about that—after we know we have enough food to eat, water to drink, and air to breathe, the next thing we strive for is a safe, secure, and stable environment.

In much the same way, readers crave order, not chaos. In crime fiction, when a murder occurs or is threatened, the smooth order of things is disrupted. The antagonist has betrayed society's rules, and sometimes the betrayal is personal. Citizens are fearful and confused. By the end of the story, though, order is restored. Good triumphs over evil. The guilty are punished. Personal sacrifice is rewarded. All is well with the world, at least for one moment in time.

Here's what this psychological truth means to you as a writer: You must create protagonists that your readers care about, then force those characters to deal with confusion and betrayal. Your readers will root for their success, and they won't be able to put the book down until the good guy comes out on top. This approach isn't trite. It is a formula for success based on most readers' deeply held beliefs, values, and instincts. In fact, Dr. Maslow would say we're born this way. Further, since this story arc transcends genres, you can easily adapt it to your work no matter what you're writing.

The following books showcase how this principle—that readers abhor confusion and betrayal and revere stability—has been used successfully in a variety of genres.

Breaking Free From a Spy's Web

Consider James Grady's 1974 novel, *Six Days of the Condor* (also discussed in chapter two). The protagonist, a brilliant CIA researcher who is a member of an elite group charged with analyzing the plots in mysteries and thrillers, stumbles on a real-life conspiracy. While he is unexpectedly out of the office, assassins storm the building and kill all his co-workers. This appealing, smart protagonist must fight unknown enemies in a desperate effort to save his own life and bring the criminals to justice. The entire story revolves around confusion and betrayal.

Although the movie version (*Three Days of the Condor*) is quite different from the book, the core themes are identical: A solid citizen doing the right thing is betrayed by the very people he should be able to trust the most. The hero is cast into a world as befuddling as a carnival fun house where the out-of-whack mirrors challenge his balance, perceptions, and self-confidence. He can't tell the good guys from the bad guys, and he has no spy craft or military training to call on—he's a researcher, not an operative. Since readers (and viewers) care deeply about this good man, this brainy hero, this everyman, they share his anxiety and fear as he struggles through the many obstacles keeping him from the truth, and thus, from salvation. When he ultimately succeeds in vanquishing evil, stability returns and readers breathe a hearty sigh of relief.

Weighing an Ethical Dilemma

The 1996 literary novel, *Primary Colors*, by Anonymous (later identified to be journalist Joe Klein), is a roman à clef—a work of fiction based on fact. The story, which follows a presidential campaign, was, according to some critics, based on President Bill Clinton's first run for the presidency.

Using a chronological bookend structure, *Primary Colors* begins and ends with the narrator's observations about the candidate's handshakes and how different grips, durations, and pressures communicate different messages. It's written from the narrator's point of view, in the first person.

Overall, the book investigates the ethics of winning at all costs. Thematically, it poses the question about whether the end can ever justify the means. After all, a presidential candidate can have the best plans and all the leadership skills in the world, but if he doesn't win, all of his good intentions are for naught.

The narrator is a young idealist just joining the campaign. As he witnesses lie after lie, misrepresentation after misrepresentation, and unseemly conduct at odds with the candidate's squeaky clean public persona, he becomes more and more disillusioned. By the end of the novel, he must choose whether to make what feels much like a deal with the devil by supporting the candidate or fight what he's certain is a losing battle to preserve righteousness by revealing the truth.

Primary Colors follows this young man's soul-searing crisis of conscience as he struggles to balance the conflicting imperatives of loyalty and truth telling. It's easy to say you should always tell the truth, but if you're a trusted advisor who agrees to keep a confidence, isn't revealing that secret intrinsically disloyal? Isn't it, in fact, a form of betrayal? Or is the deeper betrayal asking someone to shield you in the first place? If so, does that initial betrayal release you from your commitment to keep everything confidential?

Other questions the characters must face include the following: Are all lies equal? Is it all right to lie about personal issues, like sex, for instance, but not about public issues, like whether you'd allow gay people to serve openly in the military?

The campaign worker must decide which decision will lead to the stability he yearns for, endorsing lies and helping the candidate he supports get elected, or telling the truth, which will almost certainly give the election to the opposing party. Since the two central characters, the candidate and the campaign worker, are both likeable, readers (and viewers of the movie that came out two years after the book was published), empathize with both men. Most people can see and understand both sides of these epic issues, ensuring that the story resonates with a wide audience.

Channeling Inner Turmoil

In Paula Hawkins's 2015 suspense novel *The Girl on the Train*, one of three narrators, Rachel, thinks her general befuddlement is a consequence of too much alcohol, but it's not. Over the course of the novel, Rachel becomes involved in a missing person investigation. She doesn't know what's happening much of the time, yet she's driven to continue digging. In doing so, she helps solve the mystery—and discovers the truth about her own situation.

None of the narrators in *The Girl on the Train* are likeable in a traditional sense. Rachel is a mooch and a drunk. Megan betrays her husband. Anna is a home wrecker. They all lie. Yet the author succeeds in getting us to care what becomes of them. This ability to create empathy without pathos is tough to accomplish. Success comes from the fact that each of the women wants to be better than she is, and readers can relate to that unspoken, inner ambition. Each strives to find her unique self amid a cacophony of conventional expectations. Each struggles to find her place in the world.

Since we care about the outcomes of each of their situations, we experience their confusion alongside them. We share their anxiety. We feel their despair when they realize how they've been betrayed. At the end, when two of the three women succeed in fighting their way out of the quagmire that had threatened to drag them into oblivion, we celebrate their endurance and tenacity and we wish them well.

Fighting for Faith

Patton Dodd's 2004 memoir, *My Faith So Far: A Story of Conversion and Confusion*, follows a young man in his search for faith. Dodd's experiences run the gamut from living in an über-conservative and structured religious community to his more progressive personal reflections. Throughout his story, he tells the truth about his struggles, his puzzlement, and how he felt betrayed by the cultural trappings of traditional Christianity.

Dodd's quest is patently heartfelt. His stories are sincerely wrought. He expresses his seemingly contradictory experiences with emotional candor. He details his initial fervent conversion and subsequent doubts, his acquiescence and denial, and his euphoria and depression with precision and simplicity. His hunt for definitive answers resonates loudly and clearly, and his commitment to finding the truth is touching. Confusion leads to clarity; betrayals lead to trust.

FAQ

Q: Confusion and betrayal seem a lot like twists/reversals/moments of heightened danger (TRDs, discussed in detail in chapter three). How do they differ?

A: Confusion and betrayal aren't synonymous with TRDs, but they lead to them. They can serve as underpinnings in your plot or story line. Confusion and betrayal are prime motivators. Since people hate confusion and dread betrayal, they're motivated to do whatever it takes to avoid those states. As you think about how to confuse and betray your protagonist, remember that what comprises confusion or betrayal depends on the person's interpretation of events. Sometimes this concept of interpretation itself drives the plot, as in Karin Altenberg's 2014 novel *Breaking Light*. The young protagonist, Gabriel, is convinced he has betrayed his best friend, Michael. But as the years pass, his views shift. He comes to see that it was he who was betrayed, not the other way around. When acceptance, love, or affection is conditional, and you're not meeting those conditions, your only hope to win approval is to pretend, to follow the party line. Gabriel comes to recognize that conditional love is itself a kind of treachery.

A JOURNEY OF DISCOVERY

Confusion is in the eye of the beholder. What's simply smart business to one person confuses another and may represent a betrayal. To capitalize on this powerful suspense-building strategy, you need to know exactly what confuses your characters and what, in their eyes, represents a betrayal. You can't generalize or homogenize. The issues you raise must align seamlessly with your characters' innermost thoughts, fears, anxieties, beliefs, values, and expectations. Figure 9.1 lists more than two dozen questions about your characters to ensure you understand them enough to use this powerful strategy.

Before embarking on the complex journey of analyzing your own characters, it can be useful to answer the questions for characters you know well. Choose a book that you admire from your genre and analyze its characters with the questions in Figure 9.1. The answers will reveal the characters' layered complexities and how they segue into suspense.

To demonstrate this approach, I chose the two detectives in Rex Stout's traditional Nero Wolfe mystery series, Nero Wolfe and Archie Goodwin. The series spanned forty years, from 1934's *Fer-de-Lance* to 1975's *A Family Affair*, and includes more than seventy books and novellas, many of which are still in print. Because I know the opus well and admire the characters, they're a logical choice for my analysis.

After reviewing Figure 9.1, ask yourself how you might use this information in your own writing.

FIGURE 9.1: KNOW YOUR CHARACTERS

Name and Occupation
Nero Wolfe: private detective
Archie Goodwin: private detective

Physical appearance and age:
Nero Wolfe: Mr. Wolfe is white. He is about 5'10" and he weighs a seventh of a ton. He's in his fifties.
Archie Goodwin: Archie is white. He's just shy of 6 feet and handsome, although he thinks of himself as nice looking rather than drop-dead gorgeous. He's fit.

Is your character essentially a good person, or is he intrinsically flawed? What led to her developing into the person she is today? Was he reared in a home with traditional values but rebelled

against those values? Did she overcome years of abuse as a foster child?
Nero Wolfe: Mr. Wolfe is heroically good. His word is his bond. He was reared in Montenegro and fought in several wars. He is a patriotic American, a naturalized citizen.
Archie Goodwin: Archie is from Ohio. He was raised with traditional American values.

Where does your character live, and how does he feel about living there?
Nero Wolfe: Mr. Wolfe lives in a New York City brownstone he owns. He rarely leaves, and never on business.
Archie Goodwin: Archie lives in Mr. Wolfe's brownstone. This environment suits him to a tee.

Describe your character's key relationships. Is he married? Family oriented? A loner? Gay? Who's her best friend?
Nero Wolfe: Mr. Wolfe is determinedly single. He considers women dangerous. He counts on Archie to interpret their behaviors for him. His best friend is Marco Vukic, whom he's known since they were children together in Montenegro. Marco is killed in *Black Mountain*.
Archie Goodwin: Archie loves women. He dates a lot, although his main squeeze is Lily Rowan (a recurring character). Archie has a group of friends with whom he spends time. He plays in a weekly poker game.

What are your character's hobbies or favorite leisure activities?
Nero Wolfe: Mr. Wolfe is a voracious reader.
Archie Goodwin: Archie has varied interests, most notably dancing and baseball.

Does your character have any pets? If so, what? If not, why not? How does your character feel about pets?
Nero Wolfe: No, although in *Die Like a Dog*, Mr. Wolfe temporarily adopts a black lab, noting the breed has the largest brain of any canine species.
Archie Goodwin: No. Although it's never explicitly discussed, I infer that Archie would shy away from the responsibility.

Name some quirks, idiosyncrasies, or flaws in your character's behavior or personality that pop up in the story or affect the action. For instance, does he drink too much? Carry a red rabbit's foot for luck?

Nero Wolfe: Mr. Wolfe is blunt and unconcerned with people's opinion of him. He is brave. When thinking with all his brainpower, he does what Archie calls his "lip exercise," pushing his lips out, then pulling them in. During a lip exercise, Mr. Wolfe is so concentrated, he wouldn't notice a trumpet blaring.

Archie Goodwin: According to Mr. Wolfe, Archie spends too much money on clothes.

What kind of vehicle does your character drive? Or does he not drive, and if not, why not?

Nero Wolfe: Mr. Wolfe doesn't drive. He is terrified of moving objects like cars, trains, and planes.

Archie Goodwin: Archie drives a Heron sedan owned by Mr. Wolfe.

What's in your character's refrigerator?

Nero Wolfe: Mr. Wolfe is a gourmet with a live-in chef (a recurring character named Fritz). His refrigerator is always well stocked with things like thyme honey imported from Greece. He drinks copious amounts of beer.

Archie Goodwin: Archie eats most meals in the brownstone, so he doesn't have a refrigerator of his own. When Archie eats out (say when he's being questioned at the police station) he orders corned beef sandwiches and milk.

What motivates your character to do whatever it is you have her doing? If the character is a police officer, for example, why did he join the force? If she's a caterer, what drives her love of food?

Nero Wolfe: Mr. Wolfe hates to work. His only motivation is money, although sometimes he takes a job to fulfill a moral obligation or to preserve his self-esteem.

Archie Goodwin: Archie thinks of himself as a working man, but he also likes puzzles and wants to do the right thing. Often he bullies Mr. Wolfe into taking on a job because a pretty young woman is involved.

Summarize her values. Is your character religious? Does she operate under "situational ethics," or is she a black-and-white sort of gal?

Nero Wolfe: Mr. Wolfe is not religious. He is motivated by a righteous belief in the truth. That said, he's not above a little breaking and entering, if needed, and he sometimes finds it necessary to lie to the police.

Archie Goodwin: Archie is not religious. He is motivated by a righteous belief in the truth. That said, he's not above a little breaking and entering, if needed, and he sometimes finds it necessary to lie to the police.

What's your character's favorite food? Where does this preference come from? Is it comfort food Mom used to prepare? A new flavor discovered as an adult?
Nero Wolfe: This is a tough one because Mr. Wolfe enjoys a wide variety of foods. One possibility is saucisse minuit, discussed in *Too Many Cooks*.
Archie Goodwin: After more than a decade eating at Mr. Wolfe's table, Archie is developing a palate, but there is no one favorite food that comes to mind (other than corned beef sandwiches and milk, mentioned before).

What really irks your character?
Nero Wolfe: Women who are hysterical, and he believes that even the calmest of women is always on the verge of hysteria.
Archie Goodwin: Nothing. Archie is even-tempered. He might get angry, but he's never irked.

Is your character educated? Is it a formal education?
Nero Wolfe: Mr. Wolfe is a genius and incredibly well-read. There is no reference to a formal education.
Archie Goodwin: Archie graduated high school in Ohio. He reads *The New York Times* daily, and on one occasion, a professional journal.

How does she dress? Is your character a clotheshorse? Or does she dress mostly for comfort?
Nero Wolfe: Mr. Wolfe always wears suits; usually they're brown. His shirts are typically yellow, his favorite color.
Archie Goodwin: Archie is a clotheshorse.

How much money does your character earn? Is he frugal? How much does he have in the bank?
Nero Wolfe: Specific numbers are rarely mentioned, but one can easily infer that Mr. Wolfe earns in the middle six figures.
Archie Goodwin: Specific numbers are rarely mentioned, but one can easily infer that Archie earns a comfortable middle-class living.

Does your character have any ailments or disabilities?

Nero Wolfe: Only obesity, although one could conjecture that his disinclination to leave his house is a form of agoraphobia.
Archie Goodwin: No.

What's your character's background? Is that relevant?
Nero Wolfe: Mr. Wolfe is from Montenegro and his ethnic background comes up frequently. He is proud to be an American, and that comes up frequently, too.
Archie Goodwin: Archie hails from Ohio. His background is occasionally mentioned, but it's not central to the stories.

What are some pet phrases or quirky sayings your character uses?
Nero Wolfe: Pfui. Satisfactory. Very satisfactory. Indeed.
Archie Goodwin: None.

What would be your character's ideal vacation? Does she take it? If not, why not?
Nero Wolfe: Mr. Wolfe hates to travel. He is content staying at home.
Archie Goodwin: Archie spends a month or so each summer at Lily Rowan's Montana ranch. He often weekends at her summer place in Westchester County. Once they went to Norway on vacation.

Name an underlying theme that directs your character's life. Is it a desire to fit in? A determination to clear his name? A need to find her biological mother? To reconnect with the man of her dreams? To return to Earth?
Nero Wolfe: Mr. Wolfe doesn't like most people and has organized his life so he doesn't have to interact with them. He considers the ten thousand orchids in his rooftop conservatory his concubines.
Archie Goodwin: Archie is a man about town but only within the confines of acceptable behavior.

What else?
Nero Wolfe: Mr. Wolfe admires Archie for his strengths. He doesn't try to change him or mold him in his own image.
Archie Goodwin: Archie is the first-person narrator of the stories. He writes the "reports" in his room on his own typewriter.

What is likely to confuse your character?
Nero Wolfe: Having to interact with a smart, savvy woman. (See *Death of a Doxy*, *Gambit*, and *Plot It Yourself*, among others, for examples of Mr. Wolfe doing just that.)

Archie Goodwin: Not speaking the language, literally (see *The Black Mountain*) or figuratively (see *Death of a Dude*). Being in a situation requiring a level of brainpower he lacks (see *Second Confession* and *The Silent Speaker*).

What will your character perceive as a betrayal?
Nero Wolfe: Archie taking a bribe. (It never happens, although Mr. Wolfe and Archie use the gambit more than once to fake out a criminal. (See *Some Buried Caesar* and *The Silent Speaker*.) One of his employees taking advantage of their relationship (see *A Family Affair*).
Archie Goodwin: Someone putting Mr. Wolfe at risk. (See *The League of Frightened Men*.)

As you can see, Nero Wolfe and Archie Goodwin each possesses characteristics the other lacks, yet because they share core values, the differences are minor in the final analysis. They arrived in New York via different paths and became private detectives for different reasons, yet they mesh seamlessly. Taken together, they're an unstoppable team.

- Mr. Wolfe has the brains. Archie has the brawn.
- Mr. Wolfe hopes never to leave his house. Archie loves running around.
- Mr. Wolf solves crimes by thinking. Archie solves them by doing.
- Mr. Wolfe doesn't understand women. Archie knows what makes women tick.

By understanding the dynamics between Nero Wolfe and Archie Goodwin, I'm better able to understand what I need to do with my own characters. Note that the final two considerations in Figure 9.1 relate to confusion and betrayal. If I want to confuse Mr. Wolfe, I would create a powerful female character. She wouldn't defer to men, but instead would assess them individually. This approach mimics Mr. Wolfe's process of dealing with people, but he doesn't expect this kind of rationality from wom-

MASTERING SUSPENSE, STRUCTURE, & PLOT

en. The scene would be designed to accomplish three things: (1) reveal that the woman isn't intimidated by Mr. Wolfe; (2) reveal that Mr. Wolfe is intimidated by the woman, initially, at least; and (3) reveal information that moves the plot along.

And that's good writing.

TO UNDERSTAND THE POWER OF BETRAYAL AND CONFUSION, LOOK TO THE CLASSICS

Themes involving betrayal and confusion run through much of classic literature, including plays. Euripides' tragedy, *Medea*, first produced in 431 BCE, tells the story of Medea's descent into madness after her husband, Jason, leaves her for a younger woman. Vulnerable, muddled, and volatile, Medea kills her own children. The psychological integrity of the play makes it feel quite modern despite having been written nearly 2,500 years ago.

Similarly, to see how betrayal directs plot and changes people, you can't do better than Shakespeare's *Macbeth* and *Hamlet*. For examples of the consequences of confusion, consider reading *A Midsummer's Night's Dream* and *A Comedy of Errors*. *A Comedy of Errors*, for example, is about confusion and alleged betrayal. Two sets of twins are inadvertently separated at birth. Mistaken identities lead to farcical misunderstandings. At the end, when the twins are reunited, stability is restored and celebrations abound.

Anthony Trollope's six Palliser novels (published from 1864 to 1879) are enjoying renewed popularity, and it's easy to understand why. Trollope nails human interactions. The series is about politics, but politics, Trollope believed, is all about people. His assessment of political success, which many believe resonates as strongly today as it did 150 years ago, was that it depends more on connections and backroom deals than wisdom or righteousness.

Trollope's politically savvy characters measured success not by looking at legislation passed, but by comparing levels of status and power. One of the ways they did this was by listening to scuttlebutt; that is, they used gossip as a barometer of public opinion, much as is done today.

The information the politicians gleaned was usually contradictory, no surprise, since we're talking about rumors and innuendo. To further complicate the issue, assessments about truth telling were often based on who was most sexually attractive. (You'll note that this is a similar phenomenon to the halo effect, discussed in chapter seven.) Everyone was confused. The threat of betrayal lurked around every corner.

IDENTIFY KNOWLEDGE GAPS

Knowing your characters well enables you to write moments of confusion and betrayal that will reach your readers with striking perspicuity. For instance, in 2008's *The Murder Notebook*, author Jonathan Santlofer invites readers to experience a character's anguish, his torment riddled with confusion. This excerpt is a quintessential example of showing, not telling. Note Santlofer's use of precise language, crucial in describing abstract concepts like emotions.

> He lumbers across the room, one bad ankle aching and swollen, entire body sluggish from too much medication, and whacks the side of the set. A man speaking in Spanish to a woman in so much makeup he thinks her face is made of plastic, and he's right: It melts like a multicolored candle, red lips oozing out the bottom of the TV set right onto the floor. He stares at the puddle until it disappears and knows it isn't real because there she is, the woman with all the makeup, back on the screen.
>
> He sags into bed, looks up at a naked lightbulb, snippets of his life playing like the Spanish soap opera: wife, daughter, outbursts, arguments, full-scale war, sad sacred moments that no longer belong to him, and he sees himself falling, over and over.

This kind of spare, incisive writing can be achieved only when you understand your characters' deepest needs and desires and fears, when you know what they cherish and what they despise.

Figure 9.2 examines what we know and where we have knowledge gaps with the protagonists in our two case studies. You'll notice several gaps in this analysis. This process, therefore, becomes a kind of safety net, ensuring I know enough about my characters to convincingly write my books.

Completing this character analysis helps you pinpoint knowledge gaps regarding your own characters. You think you know them well, and perhaps you do. It's possible, though, that you only know them in certain ways. Taking the time to complete the chart for your primary character(s) helps you discover what you don't know. Once you identify the gaps, you can close them. Often this process leads to insights that take your story or characters in previously unthought-of directions. When it comes to aligning confusion and betrayal with your specific characters' most deeply held thoughts, desires, and beliefs, knowledge truly is power.

FIGURE 9.2: IDENTIFYING KNOWLEDGE GAPS

Premise:
Case Study #1: Kayla is a single noncustodial parent who is being stalked, maybe by her ex-husband. Her mother is sinking into dementia. Her sister is profoundly unloved.
Case Study #2: Al is a gambler who feels assaulted from all sides with his own struggles and with family members who are not helping him cope.

Occupation:
Case Study #1: Office manager
Case Study #2: High school math teacher

Physical appearance and age:
Case Study #1: Knowledge Gap. I have only a vague image in my mind's eye. Kayla is in her late twenties, pretty, but not spectacular. She doesn't stand out.

Case Study #2: Knowledge Gap. I have only a vague image in my mind's eye. Al is in his early fifties, of average height, a little chubby, and bald.

Is your character essentially a good person, or is he intrinsically flawed? What led to her developing into the person she is today? Was he reared in a home with traditional values but rebelled against those values? Did she overcome years of abuse as a foster child?

Case Study #1: Kayla grew up in a family riddled with anger and tension. Dad was mostly absent. When he was home, he was disengaged. Mom was bitter. Her sister dreamed of travel, fame, and glamour and resents that none of her dreams came true. Kayla escaped from home by marrying her high school boyfriend. Five years into a bad marriage, she began drinking heavily. Within a year of their divorce, she lost custody of her children. The book is set a year after that. Kayla has been sober for nine months. Getting her kids back is a driving force in her life.

Case Study #2: Al grew up pampered and cherished, the only son in a paternalistic, traditional family. He began gambling in high school, betting on fantasy football, and graduated to poker in college. He was good at it and earned a fair amount of money, enough so he wasn't dependent on his family for spending money. He relished the freedom. He doesn't recall when gambling stopped being fun, probably about the time he stopped winning. Once he was out of college, he started playing at casinos, and for the first time, he ran into players who were better than he was. He is good at keeping secrets, a skill he learned from his sister, older than him by five years and a wildcat.

Where does your character live, and how does he feel about living there?

Case Study #1: An affluent suburb in New Jersey chosen by her ex-husband. She hates it. She wants to move to Florida.

Case Study #2: Santa Monica, California, not far from the house where he was born. He loves it.

Describe your character's key relationships. Is he married? Family oriented? A loner? Gay? Who's her best friend?

Case Study #1: Kayla has no friends. She lost them all during her marriage since she wasn't allowed to go out by herself in the evening. She thinks of herself as a loner. She's proud that she doesn't need anyone.

Case Study #2: Al is gregarious and a genuine people person. He stays in touch with his students after they graduate. He's the life of every party. He is sincerely interested in people. He knows that his family wishes he were a little less available to everyone else so he'd have more time for them.

What are your character's hobbies or favorite leisure activities?

Case Study #1: Knowledge Gap. I haven't thought about this.

Case Study #2: Other than gambling, Al enjoys golf and is known to cook a mean backyard barbeque.

Does your character have any pets? If so, what? If not, why not? How does your character feel about pets?

Case Study #1: Knowledge Gap. Kayla doesn't have a pet now, but I don't know how she might feel about pets in the future. She might get a dog if her kids want one. I think she'll overcompensate in her efforts to get back into her kids' good graces.

Case Study #2: Al has a golden retriever. His name is Bo. He's seven years old.

Name some quirks, idiosyncrasies, or flaws in your character's behavior or personality that pop up in the story or affect the action. For instance, does he drink too much? Carry a red rabbit's foot for luck?

Case Study #1: Kayla is hypersensitive, always on the lookout for trouble. She had to develop this skill as a child to know when to leave before her parents' anger caught her in its snare. She aches for a drink every day. Her drink of choice was vodka.

Case Study #2: Knowledge Gap. I haven't thought about this at all.

What kind of vehicle does your character drive? Or does he not drive, and if not, why not?

Case Study #1: A family sedan that she hates. She wants a small SUV.
Case Study #2: A big SUV.

What's in your character's refrigerator?

Case Study #1: Knowledge Gap. I haven't thought about this at all.
Case Study #2: Knowledge Gap. I haven't thought about this at all.

What motivates your character to do whatever it is you have her doing? If the character is a police officer, for example, why did he join the force? If she's a caterer, what drives her love of food?

Case Study #1: Kayla got a nothing office job right out of high school, part of her escape plan. She worked her way up to office manager but is probably not going to go further at her current company. During the years she spent drinking heavily, she almost lost her job several times. When she moves to Florida, she hopes to attend paralegal school, and maybe someday law school, although she hesitates to let herself dream that big.

Case Study #2: Al loves being the center of attention, and he's great with numbers. Teaching math is a perfect fit for him. He applies for every job at community colleges in the area, though, not because he doesn't love his current job at the high school, but because he needs more money.

Summarize her values. Is your character religious? Does she operate under "situational ethics," or is she a black-and-white sort of gal?
Case Study #1: Kayla wishes she had faith, but she doesn't, and secretly, she doesn't understand how anyone can. She's self-contained and self-reliant. She sees the truth and fairness in black-and-white terms.
Case Study #2: Al attends church but never thinks about religion. It's just part of what you do. Al is all about situational ethics. He's a master at positioning what he wants to do so it fits snugly with what he's expected to do.

What's your character's favorite food? Where does this preference come from? Is it comfort food Mom used to prepare? A new flavor discovered as an adult?
Case Study #1: Knowledge Gap. I haven't thought about this at all.
Case Study #2: Knowledge Gap. I haven't thought about this at all.

What really irks your character?
Case Study #1: Knowledge Gap. I haven't thought about this at all.
Case Study #2: Knowledge Gap. I haven't thought about this at all.

Is your character educated? Is it a formal education?
Case Study #1: Kayla is a high school grad. She was always a good, if uninspired, student. She was serious and diligent.
Case Study #2: Al has a master's degree in education. His undergrad degree was in math, with an education minor. He got his master's so he could get a raise at his job.

How does she dress? Is your character a clotheshorse? Or does she dress mostly for comfort?
Case Study #1: Kayla wears plain clothes in neutral colors, as if she wants to avoid standing out.
Case Study #2: Al is a sharp dresser. For example, his shirts feature monograms on the cuffs.

How much money does your character earn? Is he frugal? How much does he have in the bank?
Case Study #1: Kayla earns $57,000. She is extremely frugal. She is assiduously saving for her proposed move to Florida. She has $17,314 in the bank.

MASTERING SUSPENSE, STRUCTURE, & PLOT

Case Study #2: Al earns about $55,000 from his teacher's salary and another $12,000 from teaching summer courses at the local community college and tutoring. He has nothing in the bank.

Does your character have any ailments or disabilities?
Case Study #1: No.
Case Study #2: No.

What's your character's background? Is that relevant?
Case Study #1: Kayla's ethnicity includes a mixture of Irish and English, with a smattering of French thrown in. She feels no connection to her heritage.
Case Study #2: Al is German on both sides. When asked about his affinity to his German background, he replies that he likes beer.

What are some pet phrases or quirky sayings your character uses?
Case Study #1: Knowledge Gap. I haven't thought about this at all.
Case Study #2: "If you were a triangle, you'd be acute one." "People who do their math homework in pen are fearless."

What would be your character's ideal vacation? Does she take it? If not, why not?
Case Study #1: Knowledge Gap. I haven't thought about this at all.
Case Study #2: At a casino. Any casino, anywhere. On a cruise ship with a casino.

Name an underlying theme that directs your character's life. Is it a desire to fit in? A determination to clear his name? A need to find her biological mother? To reconnect with the man of her dreams? To return to Earth?
Case Study #1: Kayla wants to feel safe. She craves stability.
Case Study #2: Al wants to be a big fish, and he doesn't mind that he's swimming in a small pond. He strives to avoid problems and ill will, which is why his current situation is so challenging for him.

What is likely to confuse your character?
Case Study #1:

- Kindness from her ex-husband
- Sympathy from her sister
- Romantic attention from a new man

Case Study #2:

- Watching another gambler on a winning streak, since he can't shake his slump. Given that Al dismisses the role of luck in gambling, he's mystified about what the other guy is doing that he's not.
- His son apologizing for getting arrested
- His father moving out, leaving him a note saying he was tired of being treated like an invalid

What will your character perceive as a betrayal?
Case Study #1:

- Her husband bad-mouthing her to her children
- Her sister telling her it's no wonder your husband left you—you're fat and stupid
- The police thinking she stole her own purse

Case Study #2:

- The neighbor with whom he's been flirting telling his wife about their relationship
- His son lying to the police that Al beats him in order to get back at him
- Al's sister convincing his father to make her his sole heir

WRITE BASED ON A DEEP UNDERSTANDING

As you answer the questions contained in Figure 9.3, think about how you might integrate this information into your stories. If you create a character who's a vegetarian, for instance, you can have a so-called friend betray her by not revealing there's beef broth in her vegetable soup. Remember, the more specific and idiosyncratic your character's attributes, the more robust and engaging your plots. Don't be vague, overly general, or ordinary.

Keep in mind there's no one right answer. You can take your characters (and your stories) in countless different directions based on your answers to these questions. Whatever path you decide to take, this exercise will help you develop the well-rounded and three-dimensional characters that lead to suspenseful stories.

FIGURE 9.3: EXERCISE: GAIN A DEEP UNDERSTANDING

• Premise:

• Occupation:

• Physical appearance and age:

• Is your character essentially a good person, or is he intrinsically flawed? What led to her developing into the person she is today? Was he reared in a home with traditional values but rebelled against those values? Did she overcome years of abuse as a foster child?

• Where does your character live, and how does he feel about living there?

• Describe your character's key relationships. Is he married? Family oriented? A loner? Gay? Who's her best friend?

• What are your character's hobbies or favorite leisure activities?

• Does your character have any pets? If so, what? If not, why not? How does your character feel about pets?

• Name some quirks, idiosyncrasies, or flaws in your character's behavior or personality that pop up in the story or affect the action. For instance, does he drink too much? Carry a red rabbit's foot for luck?

• What kind of vehicle does your character drive? Or does he not drive, and if not, why not?

• What's in your character's refrigerator?

• What motivates your character to do whatever it is you have her doing? If the character is a police officer, for example, why did he join the force? If she's a caterer, what drives her love of food?

• Summarize her values. Is your character religious? Does she operate under "situational ethics," or is she a black-and-white sort of gal?

• What's your character's favorite food? Where does this preference come from? Is it comfort food Mom used to prepare? A new flavor discovered as an adult?

• What really irks your character?

- Is your character educated? Is it a formal education?

- How does she dress? Is your character a clotheshorse? Or does she dress mostly for comfort?

- How much money does your character earn? Is he frugal? How much does he have in the bank?

- Does your character have any ailments or disabilities?

- What's your character's background? Is that relevant?

- What are some pet phrases or quirky sayings your character uses?

- What would be your character's ideal vacation? Does she take it? If not, why not?

- Name an underlying theme that directs your character's life. Is it a desire to fit in? A determination to clear his name? A need to find her biological mother? To reconnect with the man of her dreams? To return to Earth?

- What is likely to confuse your character?

- What will your character perceive as a betrayal?

You know your story, your structure, and enough about your characters to use their foibles and eccentricities to create suspense. Now it's time to write. Although it might seem counterintuitive, one of the most powerful approaches to creating page-turning scenes is to lower the volume. We'll examine this proven tactic in chapter ten.

CHAPTER TEN

WHISPER, DON'T SHOUT

> All of nature whispers its secrets to us through its sounds.
> —RUDOLF STEINER

Picture a man standing on a busy city street. He looks up, wondering what it would be like to work in a skyscraper, and he sees a woman tottering on the edge of the roof, about to jump. He yells, "Don't jump!"and runs toward the building, then, realizing he can't save her single-handedly, he calls 9-1-1. He runs back across the street so he can see, but he doesn't look up; instead, he keeps his eyes on the intersection, waiting for the rescue team to arrive, shouting, "Oh, God. Oh, God. Oh, God." Passersby stare at him as they hurry past, thinking he's a nut.

Now picture this: A man standing on a busy city street looks up, wondering what it would be like to work in a skyscraper. He sees a woman tottering on the edge of the roof, about to jump. His throat closes. He can't speak. He can barely breathe. He forces himself to calm down and calls 9-1-1, then lifts his arm, and with a trembling hand, points to the woman. Passersby pause and follow his gaze.

His screams led people to think he was crazy. His silence led people to understand his fear.

MAXIMIZE SOUND'S IMPACT THROUGH QUIET

In moments of high emotion, it's tempting to let your characters yell and shout and screech and scream, perhaps reflecting panic, maybe to encourage it. It's possible that writing a bombastic, chaotic scene is appropriate, of course, depending on the situation you're describing and the emotions you're trying to stir up. It's also possible, however, that a more measured response would communicate the chaos more convincingly.

Drawing your readers in—quietly—creates more suspenseful moments than hammering them with overly brash reveals. Don't have a character shout, "There's a gun!" Let your readers hear the click as the safety is removed.

The following excerpt is from 2006's *Consigned to Death*, the first in my Josie Prescott Antiques Mystery series. Note how the small sounds add tension and increase suspense, and how Josie's reactions to those sounds reveal key information about her character.

> As I was girding myself to step out from behind my hiding place, I heard another rustling sound and stopped cold, allowing myself to trust my instincts. I wasn't imagining things. I'd heard something, a movement, a kind of rubbing, fabric maybe, brushing against wood.
>
> In the high-ceilinged, open warehouse, sound reverberated. I thought the soft noise, a hiss or a scrape, had come from near the crates, but I might have been wrong. I pressed my back into the wall and scanned the room, seeking out something that would account for the noise, that would explain an odd shadow behind the tall stack of crates, but I saw nothing out of the way.

I swallowed. My heart was pounding so hard I was having trouble breathing. To hell with it, I told myself angrily. Probably the noise was the building settling, and I'd imagined the shadow. Silently cursing the anxiety that clung to me like barnacles to a rock, I stepped out from the corner. I was tired of jumping at shadows and fretting about small noises. No one could make me fearful but myself. Straightening my shoulders and lifting my head, I began the descent, circling down the staircase.

I heard a click and froze. The door. Someone had quietly latched the door. Were they going out? Or coming in? I stood and listened. Nothing.

SILENCE SPEAKS VOLUMES

Just as blackness is rarely fully black, so too is silence rarely silent. On the darkest night, with thick clouds shrouding the sky, lightening bugs flicker. A slender line of light appears from beneath a closet door, allowing a faint silvery glow to penetrate the blackness. In the still of an empty house, you hear the refrigerator cycling on, then off. A clock ticks. From somewhere outdoors, a dog barks. A car door slams. Wind whistles. Owls hoot. Silence is relative.

Two effective ways to build suspense are to juxtapose silence and noise. Imagine you're in a meditation class. Everyone is quiet, focused on the exercise and the teacher. A brass gong clangs. The mood is broken. Perhaps you stand up. Maybe you peek into the hall. Now picture hiking in a forest. You're enjoying the sounds of nature, the rustling as small creatures pad through the blanket of leaves, the buzzing of insects high overhead, and the calls and chirping of birds saying hello, when all at once, everything goes still. What do they know that you don't? How will you hide? Noise in the midst of silence changes everything, just as does silence in the midst of noise.

THE SCIENCE OF SOUND: CONNECTING TO READERS

Cognitive psychologists tell us that the perception of sound creates a daisy chain of reactions. When a memory is spawned from a certain sound, it leads to a specific and predictable set of reactions. Say you hear someone's voice. If you recognize the voice, a picture of that person pops into your head, which in turn fires up mental, emotional, and physical responses galore.

You can create similar responses in your readers by using Pavlovian conditioning (made famous by the nineteenth-century Russian physiologist, Ivan Pavlov), which demonstrates that if you link a neutral sound with a specific outcome, over time, you'll always associate that sound with that outcome. The sound and the outcome become unconsciously, yet inexorably, connected in the subject's mind. This linkage can breed comfort or contempt, joy or jumpiness, mania or misery, or anything in between, depending on how the subject perceives the outcome.

Consider Kayla, our protagonist from Case Study #1. She has a difficult relationship with her older sister. When Kayla was a kid, her sister teased her mercilessly about being fat and stupid. How about connecting that torment with a song? Maybe her sister loved, loved, loved "Believe," Cher's 1999 megahit, and played or sang or hummed it all the time. Now, nearly two decades later, when Kayla hears that song she reacts with familiar preteen angst. If you plant this connection early in the thriller, later when the song comes on the radio, your readers will share Kayla's visceral reaction, and they'll empathize with her determination to shed the mantle of self-loathing caused by her sister's snide bullying.

And how about Al, our protagonist from Case Study #2? Imagine how Al feels as he walks into a casino and hears a slot machine chiming, delivering its good-news message to the room. Picture him surrounded by the subdued buzz from the crowd, hearing the cheery clinks of ice and the tap-tap of chips hitting one another as they're tossed onto the green felt covering a poker table. Combined, these sounds will engender a predictable reaction in Al. His mouth will go dry. His pulse will speed up. His eyes will brighten. He's ready for action, baby. Perhaps later in the memoir, as Al is working to conquer his gambling habit, he can hear those familiar sounds and force himself to react differently than his norm, to break the disastrous cycle of linking the pleasure of gambling to those particular auditory cues.

FAQ

Q: You're devoting an entire chapter to the power of sound. Are you saying hearing is more significant than other senses, including sight?

A: Scientific and anecdotal opinions come down on both sides of that issue. Consider the work of Brown University neuroscientist Seth Horowitz. In his 2013 book *The Universal Sense: How Hearing Shapes the Mind*, he champions the unseen power of hearing. He discusses the multitude of sounds we don't notice, not only ambient noise like air-conditioning, but also sounds we create ourselves, like the soft shush of your footsteps as you pad across a carpet.

Think of how Bill, a character sitting in his breakfast nook, might react to his wife walking toward him if you described the motion as *waltzed*. *Barb waltzed across the kitchen floor.* Note that waltzing implies more than following a certain dance step—it also implies a particular attitude. How will Bill react to Barb's waltzing? Did they have a knock-down, drag-out fight last night? Is her waltz a kind of apology? Are they newlyweds deeply in love? Maybe when Bill sees Barb waltzing toward him, Patti Page's rendition of "Tennessee Waltz" starts playing in his head.

How would Bill feel if Barb *stomped* across the kitchen floor instead of *waltzed*? Stomping isn't quiet. It's angry and authoritative. It's loud. What would he do if Barb *pranced*, *loped*, *sauntered*, *strutted*, *crept*, *scurried*, or *tramped*? Each of these movement-related words comes with a set of connotations—how someone looks as they move that way, why they're moving that way, and how it sounds.

Choose the right word and your readers will hear your message loud and clear.

DESCRIBING SOUND: LANGUAGE CHOICES

Avoid Labeling Words

As we discussed in chapter four, the more sensory references you include in your writing, the more engaged your readers will be. Sensory references let readers share the characters' experiences as they happen. This is the essence of the oft-repeated admonition, "show, don't tell." Be careful, though, to avoid flagging these references with labeling terms like these:

- look
- see
- hear
- listen
- feel
- taste
- notice
- observe
- recognize
- know
- realize
- understand

While we're focusing on sound in this chapter, the principles of active writing apply to all sensory references. The before and after examples in Figure 10.1 demonstrate how eliminating labeling terminology forces you to write more active, engaging, emotionally vital stories.

FIGURE 10.1: AVOID PASSIVE LABELS

BEFORE: I raised the blind and **looked** out the window. I **saw** a man pushing a baby carriage. He waved at me.

AFTER: I raised the blind. A man pushing a baby carriage waved at me.
COMMENT: By eliminating *looked* and *saw*, the revision is tighter and more action-oriented.

BEFORE: I **saw** the gun when he leaned over to tie his shoelace.
AFTER: He leaned over to tie his shoelace. I gasped and stepped back. *Oh, my God*, I thought. *A gun.*
COMMENT: It's common to write out-of-sequence action statements. Consider rearranging them so they follow a chronological order. In this example, first he leans over, then the narrator sees the gun. Also, eliminating the word *saw* forces you to integrate more of the narrator's reaction to seeing the gun.

BEFORE: I **heard** them yelling, same as always, night after night.
AFTER: They yelled, same as always, night after night.
COMMENT: *I heard them* is distancing; *They yelled* gets you right in on the action.

BEFORE: I **listened** hard, hoping to **understand**.
AFTER: My eyes never wavered from his face. I didn't want to miss a word.
COMMENT: I'm *showing* you what it means to *listen hard*. The original version simply *tells* you what I'm doing. The revision also *shows* you what it takes to *understand*.

BEFORE: He **felt** her anger radiating across the room.
AFTER: Her lips thinned the moment she spotted him. *Uh, oh*, he thought, bracing himself. *Here comes trouble.*
COMMENT: I'm *showing* you what clued him in that she was angry.

BEFORE: I couldn't help but **notice** how old she **looked**.
AFTER: Wrinkles were etched into her sallow cheeks. Last month, her eyes were bright, twinkling even. Now they were dull. She'd aged ten years in a month.
COMMENT: I'm *showing* you why I've concluded that she's aged. I'm also providing context by describing the time frame for my comparison.

BEFORE: As soon as I read his note, I **realized** he didn't love me anymore.
AFTER: I blinked away a tear as I crumpled up his note. He didn't love me anymore.

COMMENT: *I realized* is passive, an in-your-head phrase, similar to *understand*. I'm not *telling* you she read the note and started crying; I'm showing you her reaction. *Crumpled* is a more interesting word than *read*, and it communicates attitude in addition to action. (That she read the note is implied by the fact that she crumpled it up. If she hadn't read it, it would be appropriate to write: I crumpled up the note without reading it.)

Choose Descriptors With Care

Each sound we hear comes with a set of perceptions that reaches beyond the literal meaning of the noise. If a car drives by your home with salsa music pounding, you infer certain things about the driver. Here are some examples of how various characters might describe the driver:

- thoughtless
- aggressive
- rude and disrespectful
- hip
- fun-loving
- a good dancer

In other words, when music is loud enough to disrupt your thoughts, some people go ballistic, while other people want to jump into the backseat and party down. How your characters perceive and react to noise is telling.

Find the Right Nouns and Verbs

Since it's your job as an author to find fresh ways to describe familiar things, start with nouns and verbs. Instead of simply writing *pounding salsa music*, you might add context by describing it as a/an:

- cacophony
- bludgeoning

- invitation
- party for my ears

Each of these options is thought-provoking because it takes your description in an unexpected direction. Never lose sight of the nuance of language. Words convey specific meanings, and it's crucial that you find the exact words to express the precise thought, feeling, action, or belief you intend. It's your only hope in achieving a crucial goal—to write unambiguously. Let's consider the four options listed above.

- A *cacophony* is discordant and harsh. You would never refer to music you enjoy as a cacophony.
- If I'm *bludgeoned* by the noise, I'm battered. A bludgeon is a club. It's not merely a stick—it's a weapon.
- An *invitation* is especially interesting because the word itself creates suspense. It's an incomplete thought. Readers will want to know more about that invitation. An invitation to what? A nightclub? A party? A beat down?
- The person who hears the pounding salsa music as *a party for my ears* may or may not be different from the person who hears it as an *invitation*. *A party for my ears* is indubitably positive, whereas an *invitation* might open the door to trouble. Perhaps the man driving the car with the salsa music pounding is flirting with the woman in the house. He knows that she'll recognize the music as coming from his car. He's turned it up in a show of bravado. He's challenging her to throw caution to the wind and come out and play. It's not a party for my ears, per se, but it's definitely an invitation.

Speaking of the nuance of words, even the word *pounding* should be up for debate. Perhaps there's a stronger, more specific way to describe that drive-by salsa music. Let's start with some synonyms of *pounding*.

- thumping
- grinding
- bass-driven
- thrashing

Now ask yourself how your character *feels* when listening to that pounding music. Here are some adjectives that might capture the experience:

- **SHATTERED:** communicates a strong image. If you shatter, you're in pieces, broken, destroyed.
- **SEXY:** A strong term, too, although it's vague. Can you think of how to link pounding salsa music to sexiness? How about this: "The minute the salsa music starts pounding, panties drop." The sexiness is now explicit.
- **ANNOYED:** You're not really angry. You're merely irritated.
- **READY FOR FUN:** super-vague. Is it the music that's fun? Or is it that the teenager in the house knows how much her grumpy old grandfather hates salsa music, and since she resents the heck out of him, she paid a neighbor kid to drive by with the music pounding. Since she can't be blamed for it, she gets a little fun as she watches her grandfather rant about the music in impotent fury.

It's all in the context. Context refers to more than mere background or summary; context includes the amalgam of your characters' backstories, inner motivations, and secret ambitions. Once you know what drives them to act as they do, their reactions to sound will resonate like church bells calling the faithful to pray.

Similes and Metaphors Provide Context
To take this idea even further, consider using figures of speech such as similes and metaphors to add depth to your writing.

(For more information about creating similes and metaphors, see chapter six.) The car with the pounding salsa music is about to drive by. Close your eyes and picture the moments before the car swings onto the block.

Try completing or revising this sentence: *The pounding salsa music burst into my consciousness like* _____.
(Or simply create a metaphor about the experience.)

What did you come up with? Here are a few options.

- When the devil comes to snatch you up and drag you to hell, salsa music will be pounding the whole trip down.
- The pounding salsa music burst into my consciousness, and I fell to the floor, wailing like a banshee.
- *I love you*, I thought. Every time I hear pounding salsa music I think of you, as yummy as chocolate.
- The pounding salsa music resonated across the field like one of Diomedes' battle calls.
- The pounding salsa music burst into my consciousness like a blast of thunder on a hazy summer afternoon.

Each simile or metaphor creates a different image, and as such, tells us legions about the character who experiences the sound in that way.

Choose Adjectives and Adverbs Thoughtfully

It's important to avoid adjectives and adverbs that merely compensate for weak nouns or verbs, but the well-placed and well-chosen adjective or adverb is golden. Avoid using adjectives or adverbs that merely replicate the meaning of the noun or verb or that try to add specificity to one that is overly vague. Don't write:

- Loud boom (What other kind of boom is there? Also, how loud is *loud*?)
- Sharp snap (A snap, by definition, is sharp.)

How about a "frightening boom"? *Frightening* adds another layer of meaning. Consider this scenario: Let's say you have a character who is an explosives expert. He's working with an engineering team to build a tunnel. Think about it … to him, most booms aren't frightening. In fact, generally, they're reassuring—a boom means he did his job properly. So a boom that an explosives expert finds frightening is scary indeed. Yet, even in this situation, I bet we can find a better approach because the word *frightening* is vague. How else might you describe that experience?

- Is it paralyzing? (Because even though your character works with explosives—or maybe because of it—he dreads unexpected loud noises.)
- Mortifying? (Because an explosion means your explosives expert screwed up.)
- Horrifying? (Because the explosion went off prematurely and people were hurt.)

Choosing the right descriptor ensures there's no ambiguity.

Likewise a *startling snap* informs your readers that the character wasn't expecting the noise. If your character thinks she is alone while strolling through the woods, a twig snapping is startling, for sure, and maybe terrifying. Did the twig snap when a deer stepped on a branch? Or is some person following her on purpose? (Why?) Has a hunter mistaken her for prey? Is she fit? (Can she run for it?) Here are some options to show how a few words describing a sound can make all the difference when communicating information or setting a mood.

> A twig snapped, and I hit the dirt. It was Tikrit all over again.

This allusion allows the reader to infer that the twig snapping evoked memories of when your character served in Iraq. The twig snapping reminds her of the gunshots that rang out from insurgent fire. Does your character suffer from PTSD?

> A twig snapped. It sounded just like a cracker popping at Christmas, and I nearly laughed out loud. I love Christmas crackers!

Note that linking a twig snapping to a sweet memory might be a red herring. Just because the snapping sound evokes a positive recollection doesn't mean that whatever caused the twig to snap is benign. This duality can be an especially handy tool when using an unreliable narrator.

Write About Sound with Onomatopoeia in Mind

Choosing words that imitate what they're describing—or coining them—is a powerful rhetorical technique called onomatopoeia. Words that replicate sounds add vigor to your writing by adding verisimilitude. The more believable your descriptions of sound, the more credible the scene, and the more credible the scene, the more suspenseful your writing.

Consider this excerpt from chapter six of Leo Tolstoy's 1869 epic novel, *War and Peace*, which routinely makes media and academic "top novels of all time" lists. Note that the "bright sunshine" serves as a metaphor for the men's reactions to the attacks. Also note the highly specific descriptions, like the "deafening metallic roar" and the "whistling grenade." The word *whistle* mimics the actual hissing sound of the grenade as it spins through the air.

> The gun rang out with a deafening metallic roar, and a whistling grenade flew above the heads of our troops below the hill and fell far short of the enemy, a little smoke showing the spot where it burst.
>
> The faces of officers and men brightened up at the sound. Everyone got up and began watching the movements of our troops below, as plainly visible as if but a stone's throw away, and the movements of the approaching enemy farther off. At the same instant the sun

came fully out from behind the clouds, and the clear sound of the solitary shot and the brilliance of the bright sunshine merged in a single joyous and spirited impression.

To jump-start your thinking about the versatility of onomatopoeia, consider the multitude of options that already exist. You'll find a sampler of words that replicate sounds in Figure 10.2.

FIGURE 10.2: ONOMATOPOEIA SAMPLER

argh	clunk	mutter	snort
ahem	cock a doodle doo	neigh	splash
baaaa	cough	oink	splat
bang	crackle	ouch	splatter
bash	creak	phew	splish
bam	croak	ping	splosh
bark	crunch	ping-pong	squawk
bawl	cuckoo	pitter-patter	squeak
beep	ding	plink	squelch
belch	ding-dong	plop	squish
blab	drip	pluck	sway
blare	fizz	plunk	swish
blurt	flick	poof	swoosh
boing	flop	pong	thud
boink	giggle	pop	thump
bonk	glug	pow	thwack
bong	groan	purr	ticktock
boo	growl	quack	tinkle
boo hoo	grunt	rattle	trickle
boom	guffaw	ribbit	twang
bowwow	gurgle	ring	tweet
brrrr	hack	rip	ugh
burp	ha-ha	roar	vroom
buzz	hack	ruff	waffle

ca-ching	hiccup	rumble	wallop
cackle	hiss	rush	whack
chatter	ho ho ho	rustle	wham
cheep	honk	screech	whimper
chirp	hoot	shuffle	whirr
chomp	howl	shush	whish
choo choo	huh	sizzle	whizz
chortle	hum	slap	whoop
clang	jangle	slash	whoosh
clash	jingle	slither	woof
clank	kerplunk	slosh	yelp
clap	knock	slurp	zap
clack	meow	smack	zing
clatter	moan	snap	zip
click	moo	snarl	zoom
clink	mumble	sniff	
clip clop	munch	snip	
cluck	murmur	snore	

Finding ways to describe sounds that resonate as authentic requires a keen ear and bold writing. It's easy to *tell* what someone hears. It's hard to *show* it in unexpected, yet credible, ways. When you do, you enhance your readers' experience, placing them in the scene, allowing your audio cues to evolve into suspenseful moments.

FIGURE 10.3: ADD IMPACT THROUGH SPECIFICITY

Practice rewriting the kinds of lame descriptions most of us create in first drafts. Aim to add shrewd and refined elements as you:

- Examine each verb and select an active, engaging, precise option. Try to avoid *is, are, was, were, be, being, been.*
- Convert general descriptions of sounds into specific ones.
- Add emotional and sensory details to bring the scene to life.
- Eliminate anything trite or clichéd.

BEFORE: Charlie pushed Carolyn against the wall. She screamed. He slapped her. She screamed again. He laughed in her face.

AFTER: Charlie slammed Carolyn against the bricks. She screeched, a high-pitched, wordless wail. He slapped her and she shrieked again, begging him to stop. He laughed.

DEBRIEFING:

- *Pushed* isn't weak per se; it just isn't as strong as *slammed*. A push can be soft or hard; a slam is unambiguously hard.
- *Bricks* trumps *wall*. Brick's rough texture evokes a clear, painful image; you know it hurts to hit the masonry. The wall might be merely smooth sheetrock or even rubberized padding.
- *Screamed* is also somewhat vague. Certainly *screeched* is an improvement, suggesting a startled panicky exclamation, not a generic loud shout or yell, and the addition of "high-pitched, wordless wail," brings skin-crawling authenticity to the moment. *Shriek* is also a more specific choice.
- The addition of the clause, "begging him to stop," adds crucial information.
- Deleting "in her face" eliminates a cliché.

REFLECTION: Place yourself in the moment. Be there in the room. Listen to what your characters are saying and listen harder to what they're hearing and how they're feeling. Write that.

BEFORE: Louise heard the giggles and peeked out from between the balusters. Martin was on the couch, his arm around Beth. Martin didn't look like he liked it that Beth was giggling.

AFTER:

DEBRIEFING:

BEFORE: Gunshots rang out across the field from somewhere near the church. Mickey tossed aside his shovel and ran toward the building.

AFTER:

DEBRIEFING:

BEFORE: Ms. Johnson looked around. Eighteen four-year-olds stood in single file against the wall, waiting for instructions. They didn't know how bad it was, that someone was in the hall, shooting off round after round. She'd told them not to worry, and they were young enough to believe her.

AFTER:

DEBRIEFING:

Once you've finished the exercise, reflect on your experience. How did you approach thinking through revising these scenarios? Did you follow the bulleted list of revision steps listed at the top? Were you able to add vitality and sharp descriptions to the three bland and banal examples? Did you catch how using words that identify a behavior like *look* and *hear* weaken otherwise strong sentences? Reread your revisions. Can you tighten them up even more, honing in on a few salient details that add urgency and skipping those that merely add weight?

Armed with a solid understanding of how your characters can and should experience sound, it's time to use this and our other tools to build fear and dread.

CHAPTER ELEVEN

ILLUMINATE FEAR AND DREAD

WHAT SCARES YOUR CHARACTERS?

Some people feel mildly fretful day in and day out. Other people endure a more debilitating level of anxiety. Still others live in fear, and for some, the level of fearfulness and apprehension is so severe, they experience dread. Inherent in the concept of dread is perceived inevitability. If a fear cannot be vanquished, it becomes dread.

Readers experience dread alongside characters. The shared dread becomes a kind of mythical creature, a chimera or worse that works to boost suspense even when the outcome is already known. Despite the certainty, you feel the characters' highs and

MASTERING SUSPENSE, STRUCTURE, & PLOT

lows, and you root for them. This phenomenon is apparent in memoirs of survival and triumph, such as *Apollo 13*.

Most of the world is familiar with the events surrounding April 1970's Apollo 13 mission, yet Jeffrey Kluger, co-author with astronaut James Lovell of the 1994 memoir *Apollo 13* (originally published as *Lost Moon: The Perilous Voyage of Apollo 13*), offers can't-put-it-down suspense. The book (and the movie, which came out a year later) focuses on the single-minded and disciplined effort to bring the men home safely. We know they'll succeed, yet watching the ground team's meticulous efforts using nothing but what was on the spaceship is excruciatingly suspenseful. We watched as the Apollo 13 astronauts experienced what experts tell us are three universal fears: death, abandonment, and powerlessness. As a writer, addressing these and other fears ensures your readers will feel the same terror and dread your characters do.

THE POSITIVE SIDE OF FEAR

Fear can serve as an early warning system to help us cope with danger. Given that early humans were easy prey to bigger and more agile predators, we had to develop innovative survival strategies. According to wildlife conservationist Donna Hart and anthropologist Robert W. Sussman, humans thrived for two basic reasons: We were smarter than predators, and we worked well in groups.

Hart and Sussman describe these phenomena in their 2005 book, *Man the Hunted: Primates, Predators, and Human Evolution,* explaining that as part of a group, you had a built-in safety net. Other members warned you about impending danger, and if necessary, stood beside you to fight off the attacker, as you would do for them. Since you couldn't battle these enormous and fierce creatures alone, without your group, you were essentially doomed.

While we're no longer threatened by creodonts and raptors, we seem to innately fear anything that threatens social acceptance. According to *Psychology Today*, twenty million Americans experience some form of social anxiety, or the fear of being judged, rejected, or abandoned by others. Our shared and profound fear of ostracism is actually part and parcel of being human—it's in our genes to feel it. Because this one fear—the dread that we won't be liked, accepted, or included—is so prevalent, you need to understand it, and either have your characters suffer from it or address why they don't.

WHEN YOUR READERS KNOW MORE THAN THE CHARACTERS

This dichotomy—that fear can be both positive and negative—is useful in building suspense. You can describe someone's physiological reactions to a situation, but your reader won't know whether it's a good thing or not, until you provide more information.

The Mayo Clinic tells us that when people experience anxiety, their breathing speeds up and they sweat, among other symptoms. Compare that with the physiology of excitement—the physical manifestations are the same. It's all in the eye of the beholder. If we perceive something as negative, we use a negative label to describe our emotional reaction to it; we say we're anxious. If we perceive something as positive, we use a positive label to describe our emotional reaction to it; we say we're excited. If you describe a character's reaction by *showing* it, without labeling it as positive or negative, how will readers know whether it's good news or bad? You can create suspense by leaving it up in the air until you're ready for a reveal (see chapter twelve). Even when your readers know more about the situation than your characters do, they still may not fully understand a character's reactions. Is the character reacting as the reader would, for example, or is the reaction out of whack for reasons the reader doesn't yet know or understand? Each of these scenarios can lead to complex situations fraught with suspense.

Sometimes this miscue reflects denial. Characters should feel fear, but they don't. Aharon Appelfeld's 1980 novel, *Badenheim 1939*, is set in the Austrian resort town of Badenheim, Austria, at the verge of World War II. The book tells the story of Jewish vacationers who refuse to believe the Nazis mean them harm, even after they are herded into cattle cars en route to a concentration camp. The characters are focused on their daily lives, unaware of the nightmare awaiting them. The only big-picture issue they confront is their decision to ignore the Nazi inspectors' advice to emigrate to Poland. They don't want to move to Poland because Polish Jews were considered lower class. Their worry about their status, not their extinction, is a classic example of denial. It's also a classic example of what is known as dramatic irony. Whatever term you use, the technique of allowing your reader to know more than your character builds suspense.

FAQ

Q: What about phobias? Should I treat a character with a phobia the same way as I would a character with a nonphobic fear?

A: To be classified as phobia, a fear must be excessive, persistent, and irrational. Studying up on your character's specific phobia ensures you'll present it accurately without overly dramatizing or understating reactions. Does your character have experience dealing with the phobia? Perhaps he discovered coping strategies. Maybe he knows to avoid situations that trigger the phobic reaction. Or maybe it's utterly debilitating. Any logical option will work, but you need to know enough about your character to make the right choice.

ILLUMINATE FEAR AND DREAD

In fiction, it's crucial to select an appropriate phobia and decide how the suffering character will cope. But that's only part of the battle: You also have to determine the reactions of people in his life.

For example, in Georgette Heyer's Regency romance *Cotillion*, Foster, Lord Dolphinton (known as Dolph), is so terrified of his mother, it's phobia-like. In one scene, Dolph and his fiancée Hannah Plimstock are waiting for his cousin, the Reverend Hugh Rattray, in Hugh's rectory. Every time Dolph hears a carriage approach, he's so terrified his mother has hunted him down that he dashes into a cupboard to hide. When Hugh arrives and catches Dolph hiding, he chastises him. Miss Plimstock challenges the reverend and says if it makes Dolph feel better to hide in the cupboard, so what? He isn't doing anyone any harm. This practical view of Dolph's aberrant behavior tells you as much about Miss Plimstock as it does about Dolph, and Reverend Rattray's stern reaction confirms everything you've thought about him from the start.

You should be careful not to assign someone a phobia simply as a convenience. If you need a character to *not* use e-mail, you could give him technophobia, a fear of technology. But you need to think this out carefully. If your character is a technophobe, he can't drive a tricked out electric car, for instance. You must avoid anything that seems contrived or coincidental.

There are scores of documented phobias, by the way, from ablutophobia (fear of washing or bathing) to zoophobia (fear of animals). How about a lexicographer who suffers from hippopoto-monstrosesquippedaliophobia, a fear of long words? The potential for irony is breathtaking.

A PLOT BASED ON FEAR OR DREAD

Some books' primary focus is fear and dread. F. Scott Fitzgerald once said, "Show me a hero and I'll write you a tragedy." Selecting that which we most fear or dread provides ample fodder for a rich and moving story. Figure 11.1 lists three stellar examples of doing just this, along with comments about how the elements of fear and dread come into play.

FIGURE 11.1: PLOT-BASED TALES OF FEAR AND DREAD

TITLE/AUTHOR/PUBLICATION DATE: *The Snake Pit*, Mary Jane Ward, 1946

GENRE: Semiautobiographical fiction

PREMISE: Virginia Cunningham suffers from what seems to be schizophrenia. She is institutionalized at a mental hospital where she has to cope with brutality and bureaucratic inflexibility. Despite this, she is able to get the help she needs.

COMMENTS: Both a story of one woman's struggle for sanity and an exposé of a miserable and often inhumane system, the book (and the movie, which came out two years later), created a groundswell of support for new legislation regulating the mental health industry. The title of the book refers to an ancient punishment, which was also used as torture and traces its origins back to European legends and fairy tales. The term came to be associated with mental institutions because there was some thinking among early practitioners that if mentally ill people were placed in an environment that would drive a sane person crazy, perhaps it would have an inverse effect and make them sane.

TITLE/AUTHOR/PUBLICATION DATE: *The Year of Living Dangerously*, Christopher J. Koch, 1983

GENRE: Fact-based fiction

PREMISE: In 1965, Indonesia was in the midst of political upheaval. An attempted coup led to a violent government-sanctioned, anti-communist purge. More than 500,000 people were slaughtered. The book follows a Western journalist, his Chinese-Australian cameraman, and a British woman they both love. This romantic triangle plays out amid the political turmoil. Betrayal runs rampant.

COMMENTS: The chaotic political climate echoes the internal turmoil each character faces. An important symbol used in the book is shadow puppets. In Indonesia, shadow puppet shows often feature a theme of good vs. evil, and this theme is woven throughout the novel.

TITLE/AUTHOR/PUBLICATION DATE: *Don't Stay Up Late* (Fear Street), R.L. Stine, 2015

Remember that it isn't just fear and dread that drives a plot; your character's reactions to fearful moments can also drive a story. A woman who was reared to be polite and ladylike, for example, is likely to shy away from doing anything anyone might perceive as rude. Let's say there is a man who gives her the willies. He works at a different company on a higher floor in her building. One day, an elevator stops at her floor and he's the only person on it. Some women would simply pretend they forgot something and wait for the next elevator. Your character, though, gets on anyway, lest she offend him.

FEAR CAN COME FROM ANYWHERE

What one person finds scary, others don't. Certainly there are universal fears, like death, but even those have idiosyncratic implications. For instance, one of your characters might live in constant fear of dying because he suffers from agyrophobia, the irrational fear of crossing the street.

Can you imagine how difficult it would be to navigate the world if every time you came to a street crossing you had to manage phobic symptoms? As a writer, here are some of the questions you should ask yourself before burdening your character with agyrophobia:

• What does your character's panic feel like? Does he tremble? Hyperventilate?

MASTERING SUSPENSE, STRUCTURE, & PLOT

- When he reaches the curb, what happens? Does he stop cold, frozen in a petrified stupor a yard away from the street, or does he make it to the curb, then teeter on the edge?
- Does he lie about his condition, working it so he never crosses a street alone?
- Is he ashamed? Philosophical? Proud that he's such a sensitive man?

Each phobia comes with its own set of limitations and implications. Consider the implications of characters suffering from the following phobias:

- Acrophobia, a fear of heights
  - When does the phobia kick in? At ten feet in the air? Only at the top of a roller coaster or Ferris wheel? Anything above sea level?
- Eleutherophobia, a fear of freedom
  - Freedom comes with choices, and if you've never been allowed to make them, the sudden right to do so—with all the responsibility that implies—can be terrifying.
- Limnophobia, a fear of lakes
  - Is your character phobia about all bodies of water or only lakes? Is the character phobic about all lakes or only lakes of a certain size or depth?
- Phasmophobia, a fear of ghosts
  - Many people fear ghosts, but a phasmophobe dreads seeing creatures from the afterlife. What differentiates this person is the debilitating nature of the fear. The character may be unable to attend a funeral or a Halloween party, for example.
- Scolionophobia, a fear of school
  - If your character is a scolionophobe, perhaps he or she endured terrible experiences as a child. Was she an undiagnosed dyslexic whose uncaring teacher called her stupid?
- Porphyrophobia, fear of the color purple
  - Usually color phobias are the result of a specific traumatic experience. Perhaps your character was reared in a house where corporal punishment was the rule of law. Her father donned a specific T-shirt when it was time to mete out whippings. The T-shirt was purple, and as a result, the character developed a phobia surrounding the color. Can the character eat eggplant? Use a purple Post-it Note? Will she avoid sitting on a purple chair?

No matter the phobia, enduring this kind of omnipresent fear leaves its mark. How do the other people in your character's life react? Are they supportive, or do they tease or mock the character? Do they try to understand the issue, or do they dismiss it as silly or infantile or absurd? And how does your character handle his reactions?

This kind of in-depth analysis leads to nuanced characterizations that allow you to create suspenseful plots readers can't put down. They'll feel the fear. They'll share the humiliation. Consider this example: When Pete was nine, he was about to start karate class when outside the large plate glass window, he witnessed a school bus crash into a truck. He stood with his mouth agape, his eyes fixed on the kids as they pounded on the windows trying to get out. He couldn't hear their screams, but he could see the terror in their eyes. Since that day, he can't bear to be around the color yellow. He is deeply ashamed of his xanthophobia (fear of the color yellow), and he's never told a soul how he feels, not even his mother.

Pete's in college now and dating a quiet, scholarly young woman named Nancy. He's stressing out over finals and envies Nancy's calm studiousness. The more she studies, the more anxious Pete becomes. He's in his room unable to read one more word. His roommate, Mark, comes in, also panicking about finals. Mark bitches about unfair workloads as he extracts books and supplies from his backpack. Pete spots a yellow pencil, and his vision blurs. He grasps the back of his chair to steady himself, then closes his eyes and regulates his breathing the way he's learned to do over the years, and in a moment, he's fine.

He turns away, thinking that one of these days, yellow is going to get the better of him.

Seventy pages further into the story, Pete has finished one final, which he thinks he's blown. His next one is in chemistry, his worst subject. He's moved beyond panic into molten dread. Mark comes in high-fiving—he's certain he's aced his finals. Pete feels himself sinking under the pressure. He's ashamed of his weakness. Nancy comes in his room wearing a pretty soft cashmere sweater. It's yellow.

What will Pete do next? Will he endure his inevitable, panicked reaction stoically, or will he confide in Nancy? Will he walk out of the room to avoid involving, blaming, or resenting her? Will he yell at her for egging him on even though she doesn't know about his phobia? Will he break up with her on the spot? Will he strangle her in a spasm of rage, then strip the sweater from her body and burn it?

I bet you want to know the answer, and that's the meat and potatoes of suspense.

WRITING FEAR AND DREAD

Describing how fear or dread feels to a specific person requires a clear understanding of what makes that person tick. As with every writing task, knowing what you want to express makes it easier. As we've previously discussed, don't label things. Use sensory references, select verbs and nouns that illuminate the scene and clarify people's actions, and add in occasional adjectives and adverbs.

Consider Bram Stoker's groundbreaking novel, *Dracula*. First published in 1897, this classic story is generally classified as a Gothic novel or as horror. The book tells the tale of Count Dracula's attempted move from Transylvania to England in the hopes of finding fresh blood and further disseminating the undead curse.

Dracula is told using an epistolary structure, the tale unfolding through a series of letters, diary notations, and ship log entries. These writers are the book's protagonists and narrators. (Occasionally a newspaper article is included, too. These clippings are the only information provided to the reader that the protagonists didn't witness firsthand.) In the following excerpt from chapter two notice how the geographic descriptions focus on the character's feelings of utter isolation rather than the beauty of the place. Note also his use of *repetitio*, a rhetorical trope where you repeat one word over and over again (in this case, *doors*), a reliable way to add emphasis and, in this case, a kind of quiet desperation.

> The castle is on the very edge of a terrible precipice. A stone falling from the window would fall a thousand feet without touching anything! As far as the eye can reach is a sea of green tree tops, with occasionally a deep rift where there is a chasm. Here and there are silver threads where the rivers wind in deep gorges through the forests.

But I am not in heart to describe beauty, for when I had seen the view I explored further; doors, doors, doors everywhere, and all locked and bolted. In no place save from the windows in the castle walls is there an available exit.

The castle is a veritable prison, and I am a prisoner!

Another early writer who used repetition to express fear was Wilkie Collins. Collins is often credited with inventing the modern detective novel. His books were often referred to as *sensation novels*, what we might think of as the pulp novels of the mid-twentieth century. The excerpt below comes from his novel, *Basil: A Story of Modern Life*, first published in 1852.

The protagonist, Basil, is expected to marry well. After he falls in love with a merchant's daughter, a match his father deems unacceptable, he is forced to choose between desire and fidelity. With a structure and conclusion similar to James M. Cain's *The Postman Only Rings Twice*, *Basil* is simultaneously a romance, a suspenseful tale of betrayal and revenge, and an indictment of moral laxity.

The following scene from chapter five describes the breach between Basil and his father. With sensory details, Collins astutely captures each man's unique experience with despair. As you read, notice Basil's reaction. Even though he's in the throes of grief, he is able to understand the seriousness of the situation. The ability to perceive long-term consequences in the face of heightened emotion isn't typical and reveals Basil's character.

I heard no answer—not a word, not even a sigh. My eyes were blinded with tears, my face was bent down; I saw nothing at first. When I raised my head, and dashed away the blinding tears, and looked up, the blood chilled at my heart.

My father was leaning against one of the bookcases, with his hands clasped over his breast. His head was drawn back; his white lips moved, but no sound came from them. Over his upturned face there had passed a ghastly change, as indescribable in its awfulness as the change of death.

I ran horror-stricken to his side, and attempted to take his hand. He started instantly into an erect position, and thrust me from him furiously, without uttering a word. At that fearful moment, in that fearful silence, the sounds out of doors penetrated with harrowing distinctness and merriment into the room. The pleasant rustling of the trees mingled musically with the softened, monotonous rolling of carriages in the distant street, while the organ-tune, now changed to the lively measure of a song, rang out clear and cheerful above both, and poured into the room as lightly and happily as the very sunshine itself.

For a few minutes we stood apart, and neither of us moved or spoke. I saw him take out his handkerchief, and pass it over his face, breathing heavily and thickly, and leaning against the bookcase once more. When he withdrew the handkerchief and looked at me again, I knew that the sharp pang of agony had passed away, that the last hard struggle between his parental affection and his family pride was over, and that the great gulph [sic] which was hence-forth to separate father and son, had now opened between us for ever [sic].

In this chapter, we've looked at ways to capitalize on the suspense-building potential of fear and dread. To maximize the suspense potential of those emotions, use sensory details to add authenticity to your descriptions.

Before revising the scenarios that follow in Figure 11.2, decide what the characters are truly like, where their fears reside, then steer toward that emotion. As long as fear relates to a viable internal driver, you can take the story in any direction you choose and it will work beautifully. Heighten the terror by replacing "tell" phrases (e.g., see, hear, feel, know, observe, recognize, realize, et al) with specific sensory references. Aim to write mini-scenes that communicate unequivocal fear—even from seemingly mundane events.

FIGURE 11.2: EXERCISE: WRITING FEAR AND DREAD

SCENARIO: Jim saw a burst of light and wondered if that crazy scary guy next door was shooting off fireworks. Sparks landed on his lawn. *He might be scary*, Jim thought, *but I've got to get him to stop before he burns my house down.* Jim looked back and saw Maggie.

WHAT CAN YOU IMPROVE?

- Eliminate *saw* (two usages)
- Revise the cliché *burst of light*
- Eliminate *wondered*
- Add specificity to clarify the vague description *that crazy scary guy.*
- Add specificity to *fireworks.*
- Add more about how Jim feels about talking to his neighbors.

REVISION: A neon yellow flare shot into the night sky. Sparks singed the grass five feet from where Jim stood.

Time to meet the neighbor, Jim thought. *He might be whacked out on drugs or whatever, but I'm damn sure not going to let him burn my friggin' house down.*

Jim glanced over his shoulder. Maggie stood at the kitchen sink.

He turned back toward his neighbor's house as another flare exploded, then raised his chin and said, "Let's do it to it."

SCENARIO: I didn't hear a word he said to me. All I could see was the gun, big and black and deadly.

WHAT CAN YOU IMPROVE?

REVISION:

SCENARIO: Lea heard someone laugh from inside the storage room. She wondered what was going on. It could be boy-crazy Amelia in there with her latest victim. But it also could be Batty Beatrix scaring the bejesus out of some poor schmo. Lea knew she had to go in and get the files. Her boss was waiting.

WHAT CAN YOU IMPROVE?

REVISION:

MASTERING SUSPENSE, STRUCTURE, & PLOT

SCENARIO: When I was eight, my mom and dad had a super scary fight. Dad pushed her against the wall. I slid out of my chair and hid under the table. I covered my ears and closed my eyes and prayed.

WHAT CAN YOU IMPROVE?

REVISION:

Part of writing fear and dread is not letting your readers see too much too quickly. In chapter twelve, we discuss the complex task of revealing answers slowly.

CHAPTER TWELVE

REVEAL ANSWERS SLOWLY

> ❝ If we knew all the answers, we'd be bored. ❞
>
> —JACK LALANNE

INSPIRE READER CURIOSITY

The narrative question, that key longing or conflict that forms the overarching driver of your story, shouldn't be answered all at once, or too early. Writing that engenders reader questions creates suspense.

Meredith Anthony used this technique in her short story, "Murder at an Ad Agency," which was originally published in *Ellery Queen Mystery Magazine* in 2013. Anthony leaves readers with more questions than answers, which builds gripping suspense.

> The definition of redundant: your boss keeps snakes in his office. Jenny sighed. It was midnight and the stale air-conditioned air was scented with Chinese food, bad coffee, and the faint, sweet, unmistakable stink of corruption.

In order to achieve this paradox—revelations leading to mysteries—you need to create full-blooded characters and peel away the layers of their personalities, characteristics, intentions, and/or motivations slowly. One reliable way to structure this character-driven slow reveal is through the use of an unreliable narrator.

UNRELIABLE NARRATORS CREATE SUSPENSE

An *unreliable narrator* refers to a noncredible narrator, although readers may not know the narrator isn't credible until the end of the story. Sometimes, though, the narrator is openly unreliable from the start.

The Gathering, for instance, Anne Enright's 2007 novel (which won the Man Booker Prize), opens with Veronica, the narrator, saying she wants to recount an incident from her childhood but doesn't know if she can because she isn't certain it actually happened. From that one statement, we know we can't trust the narrator, but we don't know why she's unsure about the veracity of her memory. Is she warning us that her memory is spotty simply because of the passage of time, or is there a darker reason? Does she suffer from delusions? Is she mentally ill? In *The Gathering*, Veronica has to investigate secrets and lies to uncover the truth. If a character's version of events cannot be trusted, the reader has to wait for the plot to unfold before the truth is revealed.

From a writer's point of view, you're on solid ground if you have a character struggle with remembering things. The Innocence Project, the nonprofit organization that works to exonerate wrongfully convicted prisoners through DNA testing, reports that mistaken eyewitness testimony is a factor in nearly three-quarters of their successful cases. Further, about a third of these exemplars relied on more than one incorrect eyewitness testimony. There is no implication (at least most of the time) that eyewitnesses purposely lie. Memory is dicey.

Remembering something isn't like rewinding a movie that lives in your head. Cognitive psychologists report that recall comes from re-creating a memory, not replaying it. When re-creating a memory, we gather up the bits and pieces of sensory threads and cognitive strings and knit them together into whole cloth. If you don't have all the pieces available to call on (and we rarely do), your memory is, by definition, incomplete. So we unconsciously fill in the blanks without even knowing we're doing so. We think we recall incidents, emotions, and attitudes accurately, but usually we don't.

Further complicating the issue is that we humans tend to believe what validates our pre-existing values, so we complete our memories with what we assume is true. This process also occurs unconsciously, when traumatic incidents block all or part of a memory from forming in the first place. With the best will in the world, characters can insist they remember an event or an emotion accurately; they can speak with confidence, even with arrogance, and they can be dead wrong.

Unreliable Narrators: The Innocent

Some narrators are unreliable because they lack worldly knowledge. Perhaps they're too young to understand the context or implications of events. Huckleberry Finn, the protagonist in Mark Twain's 1885 novel, *The Adventures of Huckleberry Finn*, falls into this category. Huck is charmingly naïve, and because of his youth and inexperience, he misinterprets incidents and mis-

reads people, which result in misunderstandings, wrong conclu-
sions, and dangerous situations (like falling in with con artists).
His choices are credible because his naïveté rings true. Huck's
view of the world enables readers to consider complex issues
through innocent eyes, even when that view is a little skewed.

Since Huck's life is complicated by Tom Sawyer's determination to milk their adventures for all they're worth, Huck's innocence leads him to accept Tom's plans at face value. For example,
Tom designs an elaborate scheme to free the runaway slave, Jim,
and the suspense—and danger—are acute. Only when the truth
is finally revealed at the end of the book do we learn that Tom
already knew Jim's owner had died and willed Jim his freedom.
The delay in revealing this crucial information allows the suspense to build. The delay doesn't feel forced, though, because we
know Tom's character. It's completely in keeping with his nature that he takes unneeded risks and doesn't think about the
possible consequences.

Unreliable Narrators: The Guilty

Many unreliable narrators, however, don't set out to tell the
truth. Sometimes, as in Avi's 1992 middle school novel *Nothing But the Truth: A Documentary Novel*, the narrator lies to
cover up a weakness or a failure. Avi, (the pseudonym used by
Newbery Medal-winner Edward Irving Wortis), used an epistolary structure to tell Philip Malloy's story.

Philip, a New Hampshire track star, blames Ms. Narwin, his
ninth-grade English teacher, for his poor performance in her
class. Since he earned a D, he can't try out for track, and instead of telling his parents the truth, he says he's not interested
in track anymore. When Philip hums the national anthem and
Ms. Narwin takes it as disrespect, the issue garners national attention about the nature and role of patriotism.

An important theme running throughout the novel is the anatomy of truth. Various characters tell the truth as they know it or believe it to be, yet when the statements are taken together, we end up with, if not a lie, certainly a misrepresentation of the truth. Since there are multiple versions of the situation, readers have to wait until the book ends to learn the truth. From the start, readers might ask themselves if they can trust Philip's version of the story since they know he's lied to his parents, but they probably won't. Most people will empathize with Philip's dilemma and identify with his rebellion.

Sometimes an unreliable narrator's guilt is less ambiguous. Agatha Christie's *Murder of Roger Ackroyd* falls in this category, as does Gillian Flynn's *Gone Girl*.

Unreliable Narrators: The Biased, the Stressed, and the Mentally Ill

In order for unreliable narration to work well, you have to have clear character motivations. In Paula Hawkins's *The Girl on the Train*, published in 2015 (also discussed in chapters eight and nine), for instance, one narrator, Rachel, is unreliable because she's viewing the world through a haze of despair; another narrator, Anna, is unreliable because she's prejudiced against Rachel. Although both women think they're right—Rachel, believing that she's hopeless, and Anna, believing that Rachel is out for revenge—in fact, both women are wrong. We don't learn the truth until they trust one another, a transformation that doesn't occur until the end.

The narrator of Ken Kesey's 1962 novel, *One Flew Over the Cuckoo's Nest*, Chief Bromden, is unreliable because he's mentally ill, having been diagnosed with schizophrenia. While Chief Bromden reports events that include hallucinations, such as people expanding and shrinking and walls oozing with slime, the underlying theme of society condemning unconventional behavior in order to preserve its own standards chimes through. The dehumanizing nature of mental health care in the late 1950s is potent throughout the book, but the insidious cruelty of subtle control only becomes clear at the end, when Chief Bromden refuses to take it anymore. The final reveal, which frees him, is unexpected, and rights all previous wrongs.

REVEALS REQUIRE COMPLEX CHARACTERIZATIONS

Think about Kayla, the protagonist from Case Study #1. She's in an extraordinary situation. You'll recall from Figure 9.2, that "Kayla wants to feel safe. She craves stability." In order to have something to reveal later in the thriller, I need to add complexity to her character. What might oppose wanting to feel safe and craving stability? How about placing her in danger? Engaging in risky activities? Maybe Kayla picks up men in bars for quick hookups. Maybe she gambles with the rent money.

I'm not recommending I assign these risky activities to Kayla, but I need to layer in a secret or some unexpected behavior, so that I have something to reveal later, and one reliable approach is to look for behaviors that oppose the public or apparent characterization.

LET SUSPENSE LINGER

To execute a slow reveal, you need to follow these steps:

1. Let your readers see a specific side of your character, either positive or negative.
2. Select one or more incidents that force or allow the character to act in a way that opposes the positive or negative image.
3. Show the incident in an opposing light.
4. Reveal the truth.

Let's say your protagonist, Alisha, a former corporate IT superstar, is now a stay-at-home mom. Scenes showing Alisha canning peaches and tucking "Atta boy!" and "Atta girl!" notes into her children's lunch boxes imply that she is devoted to her husband and children. She keeps her hand in the computer world a bit by running a small online test-prep business from home.

1. Alisha's devotion is shown in her day-to-day actions. She spends hours working on her test-prep business, updating the questions, monitoring sales data, and assessing customer performance.
2. About halfway through the novel, Alisha accesses a hidden portion of her website. Using aliases and offshore decoys, she hacks into a major testing organization and steals, then sells, questions for upcoming tests.
3. Alisha meets a middle-aged man named Ian and begs him to let her quit. Ian twists a metaphorical knife in deeper, threatening her with exposure if she doesn't continue to acquire and sell the test questions.
4. Alisha goes to the FBI, confesses her role in the scheme, and explains that she first came up with the idea of stealing test questions to help her husband get into law school. To this day, he doesn't know what Alisha did. He thought that he did well on the LSAT because he studied so much, and that Alisha was terrific at helping him focus on the most important parts. Ian, Alisha reveals, is the head of security for an official testing company. When he discovered that Alisha had breached the company's computers, instead of turning her in, he forced her to continue, to sell the questions and give him most of the booty.

Clearly, Alisha did the wrong thing by stealing questions to help her husband, but she did the wrong thing for the right reason—to help the man she loved. That she didn't have a profit motive doesn't change the facts of the case, but it might make the reader think she's less bad perhaps, than if her purpose was mercenary. Certainly the dichotomy adds complexity to the character and the situation. As each plot point is revealed, our view of the character shifts and suspense is heightened.

Shifting reader perception by layering in contradictory information works well in all genres, including literary fiction. The following short story, "Mean Yellow Jacket" by G.D. Peters, which first appeared in the November 1998 issue of *Reader Break* (Pine Grove Press), uses this approach. Peters adds character-revealing information through his descriptions of Uncle Jeremiah's possessions but doesn't actually reveal the solution. Readers need to follow Christopher's lead to understand what happened and why.

> The orderly had a quizzical look on her face when I asked if Uncle Jeremiah had uttered any last words.
>
> "Mean yellow jacket," she said.
>
> "Mean yellow jacket?"
>
> "That's what he said," Virlie confirmed. "Mean yellow jacket." She was an elderly woman, and quite pleasant.
>
> "Did he say what he meant by that?"
>
> Virlie furrowed a brow, reminding me what I had asked her.
>
> "What he did after that was expire," she said, shaking her head. She spoke slowly, rubbing her hands, pausing now and then, her tongue clacking as she worked her lips together. "They call me in when it got looking bad; wasn't nothing they could do for him so I just set with him, *you* know, let it take its course. He known his number was up, see? He jes' laid there, you know, real quiet, and he had this funny smile on his face, like he had a secret under his pillow."
>
> "Is that right?"
>
> "He jes' smiled and smiled, and then started nodding his hay-ed, and he pulled a finger at me to come closer, see, so I leaned in and he smiled real wide, almost to laughing, and his hay-ed nodding up and down like he's gon' share his secret. I leaned my ear close to his mouth and he says 'mean yellow jacket,' and then he expired, you know, with that smile on his face. Damndest thing I ever seed."
>
> Virlie finished with the sheets she was changing.

"I didn't know Mista Jeremiah had no kin," she said. "You know he was a kind man. Me an' him both been here nigh onto twenty year now, see."

I thanked Virlie for everything I knew she'd done for Uncle Jeremiah, including being with him during the final moments of his life. I held her hand in mine, pressing a twenty into her palm as I turned to leave.

"Thank you, Mista Christopher," she said, "thank you kindly," as she stuffed the bill into the pocket of her apron. "Mista Christopher," she said as I was half through the doorway, "I ast' you a fayva?"

"Sure Virlie, what is it?" I said, turning back.

"This been wearing on me ever since Mista Jeremiah passed on, see. I sure 'preciate it if you ever *do* find out what he meant."

I understood. A dying man's last words, and she had no way of appreciating the secret he'd shared with her. Surely an unsettling circumstance, she only wanted some closure.

"Sure Virlie," I said, "I'll let you know."

As I drove from the Mountain View Nursing Home with Uncle Jeremiah's few remaining possessions in a cardboard box beside me on the seat, I cannot with certainty say I'd have been quite inclined to look any further into the matter if it had not been for Virlie's parting request. While Uncle Jeremiah had been known to me, he was actually a quite distant relative, the oldest brother of my cousin Rachel's grandmother on her mother's side, Rachel and I being related through our respective fathers, so Uncle Jeremiah was not actually a blood relation of mine. But being the only family member anywhere near Lancaster County it was I who got the call to make the final arrangements at the home.

Rachel put me in touch with her Uncle William Brett, who was Jeremiah's nephew. We met in Lancaster, at the office of lawyer Frank Church. Uncle William asked me to be present at the reading of the will and though I was uninterested in the legal proceedings I was curious to learn what William might have known of Uncle Jeremiah's storied past, though he was unable to shed real light upon the subject.

"What I know of Jeremiah you've already read in the magazine articles documenting his explorations," William told me. "The only other thing I know is he was involved in a big murder trial when he was a boy, mixed up in it somehow or other but it's never been solved."

The reading of the will was quite brief, the will simply providing that Jeremiah's sole possessions, which were in the cardboard box I collected at Mountain View and presented to lawyer Church, would devolve to whomsoever signed for them and carried them from the home. According to Mr. Church I now owned these possessions. I offered them to Uncle William but he declined.

"You heard Jeremiah's will same as me," he said, "it's what he provided and I respect his last wishes, whatever his reasons might have been."

As I settled onto the sofa, a 2:30 A.M. rerun of the local news flashed quietly across the television screen. On the coffee table before me was the box. I had given its contents only a cursory glance but now felt compelled to honor this life with some small gesture, if only by homage paid to his last possessions, of which I now found myself, by default, the sole heir and beneficiary.

I removed the items one by one: A shirt, obviously hand-woven from some unfamiliar fabric, whose print brought to mind an ancient Aztec civilization. And as Uncle Jeremiah had spent his adult life exploring the far corners of the globe, this did not seem unusual. A pair of worn and faded blue jeans, which upon closer inspection I found to be a very early issue from Levi Strauss & Co., perhaps from before the turn of the century; some people collect these things, but Uncle Jeremiah, apparently, just wore them. One well-worn pair of leather boots, their laces frayed but holding. One leather belt, hand stitched with a brass buckle and matching brass loop, that looked old enough to have been worn at Little Big Horn or O.K. Corral, and maybe was. One wool New York Yankee baseball cap, worn and soiled, a number "3" inked beneath its brim, faded but quite legible, and I am thinking Babe Ruth's number, but ... naah, couldn't be. One Marine Band harmonica looking as if it might be the first harmonica ever manufactured, something Uncle Jeremiah had perhaps kept from his youth early in the century. One Duncan yo-yo, circa 1961 or so, of clear green plastic, but with a new string. Virlie told me Uncle Jeremiah liked to practice his yo-yo several times a month while watching TV in the rec room. An original 1934 Breitling aviator's chronograph watch with two pushpieces, and even I recognized this to be quite valuable. At the bottom of the box were two books. One was an original hardbound edition of *The Adven-*

tures of Huckleberry Finn inscribed, apparently by the author, "to young Jeremiah, S. Clemens." The other was also a first edition, *For Whom the Bell Tolls*, also inscribed, "Jeremiah, great trip, thanks, Ernie." These were Uncle Jeremiah's possessions. The bottom of the box was lined with old newspaper, which I pried out carefully, curious to examine the date and edition. The page was from an old *Lancaster Daily Journal*, dated 1967. I perused the headlines and found an interview with Uncle Jeremiah as follows:

> **Lancaster, April 8**—On the fiftieth anniversary of the slaying of Byron Bohannon, a federal agent with the Bureau of Indian Affairs, Jeremiah Brett, 68, of Philadelphia and the only witness to the killing stated he could shed no further light on the mystery of the Ironville Two, though the original suspects are now deceased.
>
> "I testified I didn't know," Brett, an archeologist and explorer, stated. "They might still try me for perjury. I will tell you this, there were two men stood trial but I know for a fact John Pony wasn't there that night. That's all I can say right now. Maybe when I'm dying," he said, leaving historians little hope of ever learning who really killed Byron Bohannon.

Another clipping, folded neatly inside the first, was from the *Philadelphia Chronicle*, dated 1917:

> **Philadelphia, September 20**—A federal jury today acquitted the Ironville Two, Shawnee Indians tried for the April 8 killing of Byron Bohannon, agent of the Bureau of Indian Affairs who had been accused of the rape and slaying of 13-year-old Sue Standing Water, a Shawnee girl. The defendants, John Stomping Pony, 28, and Joseph Yellow Jacket, 17, were acquitted when the sole witness to the slaying, Jeremiah Brett, 16, also of Ironville, was unable to identify the killers.
>
> Under cross-examination by federal prosecutor John Barnett, Brett refused to alter his testimony, while admitting his earlier statement to authorities that he had wit-

nessed the killing. "I seen it," he testified, "but I didn't seen who done it."

Brett admitted he was a friend of Yellow Jacket, the brother of Standing Water, and of the victim herself, while refusing to answer whether she was his girlfriend. He testified he could not identify the men at the scene because it was dark.

I set my alarm earlier than usual, knowing Virlie began her morning shifts at eight. She had misunderstood his dying words. I repeated them to myself, slowly this time.

FAQ

Q: When it comes to a reveal, how slowly is too slowly? Don't you risk boring people if you slow the pace too much?

A: You raise an interesting distinction. Don't slow the pace. Do slow the reveal. Using action-oriented incidents (as opposed to reflective, private musings) speeds the pace. Writing dialogue (as opposed to exposition) speeds the pace. Adding multifaceted qualities to characters, then revealing those different facets one at a time through action-oriented incidents and dialogue maintains a quick pace while slowing the reveal.

THREE TECHNIQUES TO SET UP SLOW REVEALS

Using statements that have multiple meanings, that are open to interpretation, or that beg questions are all smart ways of encouraging reader involvement and setting up situations that lead to slow reveals. Let's take a look at each of these three techniques:

STATEMENTS WITH MULTIPLE MEANINGS: We've discussed avoiding overly general statements. To say, "She's a happy baby," is probably too generic. Adding specificity might lead you to qualifying that sentence to something like, "She always smiles!" or "She's so interested in her environment," or "She loves making eye contact." These specific versions take the bland and vague statement, "She's a happy baby," and add credibility and interest. However, sometimes, you want to write in such a way that a general statement has multiple meanings.

For instance, when a serial killer is arrested, his neighbors and co-workers often say, "He was such a nice, quiet young man." This could mean he's polite but shy. Or that he is an introvert and likes being alone. Or that he has certain rituals he follows in private. If you've let your readers peek into his private world in advance, when the neighbor utters the clichéd phrase, "He was such a nice, quiet young man," they'll nod knowingly.

STATEMENTS THAT ARE OPEN TO INTERPRETATION: As we discussed in chapter ten, your goal is to write unambiguously. Purposeful ambiguity is another issue completely. You can integrate ambiguity into your characterizations to reflect that people are not one-note creatures; we're multifaceted. You can even create a character with an alter ego, like the murder victim in Ed McBain's 1971 police procedural, *Sadie When She Died.* The woman killed was Sarah, a shrew at home, but she was also Sadie, a sex-crazed swinger, when she went out at night.

Using ambiguous sentence structure can lead to useful misunderstandings. Consider this sentence: *I saw the boy with the binoculars.* Does this mean that I saw the boy who was holding binoculars? Or does it mean that I saw the boy because I was using binoculars? You can have a listener assume one or the other of those statements, and your readers will follow along. Then later, you can reveal that the listener misinterpreted the statement, thus peeling away a layer of your slow reveal.

STATEMENTS THAT BEG QUESTIONS: Writing statements such as "The make-up didn't quite cover Lydia's black eye" allows your characters to move in any direction you choose, setting up perfect scenarios for slow reveals. To flesh out this scenario, consider this exchange between an older couple, Frank and Poppy.

"The makeup didn't quite cover Lydia's black eye," Poppy said, brushing her tears aside.

Frank slapped his armchair. "The son of a bitch."

"We don't know it was Ethan."

"Who else? You think Lydia has someone else in her life who hits her?"

"She says she fell down."

"I'll kill him. That's what I'll do, the son of a bitch. Then our baby girl won't have to worry about falling anymore."

Poppy smoothed her skirt, then met Frank's eyes. "I'll help."

Then, one hundred pages later, while Frank and Poppy are still in the planning stages, we have this: "How could she have another black eye?" Frank demanded. "Ethan's been locked up since Friday."

Each of these approaches is a reliable way to create the kinds of subtle situations and complicated characters that lend themselves to slow reveals. In the exercise that follows (Figure 12.1), see how these three techniques help you develop your stories and execute a slow reveal.

FIGURE 12.1: EXERCISE: THREE WAYS TO SET UP SLOW REVEALS

Using the information discussed in this chapter, experiment with developing the sentence "I never knew my father" into a secret-laden character or incident you can use later for a slow reveal. Consider these questions as you develop your scenarios:

• Who is speaking?
• Why didn't that person know his or her father?
• What is meant by *know*? Is this a literal statement? Metaphorical? Biblical?

APPROACH: Statements with multiple meanings

YOUR SCENARIO:

APPROACH: Statements that are open to interpretation

YOUR SCENARIO:

APPROACH: Statements that beg questions

YOUR SCENARIO:

Once you know what you want to say and why, who is saying it and how, and what these messages represent, it's time to consider the sentences themselves.

CHAPTER THIRTEEN

WRITE SENTENCES THAT WORK

 Certain brief sentences are peerless in their ability to give one the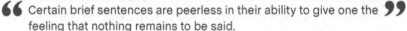
feeling that nothing remains to be said.

—JEAN ROSTAND

SAY WHAT YOU MEAN, CLEARLY

To be a successful writer, you need to adhere to the rules of conversational grammar (with obvious exceptions, such as writing in dialect). You don't to need be a grammarian, nor do you need to stick to the formal rules of academic writing, but you do need to understand the relationship between grammar and punctuation and clarity.

Note my use of the word *conversational* grammar. In formal writing, you're not supposed to start sentences with *and, but, because, therefore, so,* and other words of that ilk. That can be limiting to a fiction or literary nonfiction writer since starting sentences with those words is how people actually speak. If you want to reflect reality, it makes sense to mimic the real world. Yet starting sentences with these conjunctions and transitional expressions sometimes reflects lazy writing. Instead of starting sentences with *but*, for example, maybe you can simply drop the word. Other times, you can insert the word *though* or *however* somewhere in the sentence. The overarching lesson here is to write every sentence purposefully.

In this chapter, we'll look at how to construct sentences to maximize their suspense-producing potential.

TWO CONSIDERATIONS

Once you're ready to write, it's time to drill down to how your actual sentences should be framed. You should write sentences that average less than twenty words and move the story forward.

Complex sentences that are longer than twenty words and comprised of multiple clauses sweep readers into your world, enveloping them in a lyrical cocoon. To many readers, these long sentences relax them as surely as a walk along a quiet country lane, even when the subject matter is harsh. The length itself allows encapsulation, discovery, and reflection. Short sentences have an opposite effect, fueling tension like a dash through congested city streets. Generally you want a mix of both.

- Use long sentences to create a mood.
- Use short sentences to catapult your readers into moments of taut action.

Regardless of sentence length, it's crucial that each and every sentence moves your story forward. Skip fillers. Don't digress. Slide in a sentence or two of backstory, not more, as a way of explaining current events—no info dumps. Use dialogue to move the story along. Every line of dialogue should *do* something, not merely *say* something.

Aim for Variety in Sentence Length

Think of the twenty-word metric not as a shackle, but as a life ring. Adhering to this parameter keeps you from rambling, babbling, thinking aloud, or sinking into purple prose. Maintaining this average allows

MASTERING SUSPENSE, STRUCTURE, & PLOT

you enormous flexibility. You can write a five-sentence paragraph comprised of the following sentence lengths, for instance, and still achieve an appropriate average:

1. thirty words
2. sixteen words
3. four words
4. forty-two words
5. eight words

Add those up and divide by five and you'll see the average sentence length is right at the twenty-word standard ($100 \div 5 = 20$). Whether you monitor your work by analyzing a section, a few sentences, a paragraph, a chapter, or an entire manuscript, your goal is to maintain this average not by writing one twenty-word sentence after another, but by using a variety of sentence lengths, which creates a pleasing cadence and serves different purposes.

Do you want to encourage thought so your readers can take a quiet breath? Write a longer sentence. Do you want to have your readers charge ahead? Write a shorter sentence.

Some of the most beautiful sentences are long. Joan Didion, for example, wrote this vivid seventy-two-word sentence in her 2005 memoir, *The Year of Magical Thinking*:

> This is my attempt to make sense of the period that followed, weeks and then months that cut loose any fixed idea I had ever had about death, about illness, about probability and luck, about good fortune and bad, about marriage and children and memory, about grief, about the ways in which people do and do not deal with the fact that life ends, about the shallowness of sanity, about life itself.

Few readers would undertake reading an entire book filled with seventy-plus word sentences, but that doesn't diminish the power of this one sentence filled with soaring ideas, all of which require reflection. Yet, a sentence need not be long to be beautiful. Consider the eight-word sentence that follows Didion's seventy-two-word one. "I have been a writer my entire life."

Keep in mind that the choices you make about sentence length require more thought than merely adhering to an arbitrary number or formula; sometimes, you ignore rules or suggestions because a certain message needs to be delivered in a certain way. While Lawrence Light uses a variety of sentence lengths throughout his 2005 thriller, *Too Rich to Live*, the novel starts with short sentences that average twelve words, a surefire way to create a riveting pace. Light reveals character and implies action through varying sentence length (he even uses a fragment), and demonstrates that a series of short sentences doesn't require a staccato beat.

> Edward Danton stood in his tuxedo, listening to the hubbub of the museum benefit dinner. He never used to be the guy who would kill someone. He'd once had a pleasant smile, but now every smile was a pretense. His favorite movie used to be *Ordinary People,* but now it was *Dangerous Liaisons.* And he had been in love once, but now couldn't remember how that felt.
>
> If Edward Danton hadn't fallen in love, hard and early, he wouldn't have become a killer. Maybe a Wall Street big shot, where he could have simply terminated people's financial security. Not a killer.
>
> Tonight, Danton was going to kill a member of the Billionaire Boys Club. And the Billionaire Boy wouldn't see Danton coming.

Forward-Moving Sentences

It's tempting to add descriptive details to set a scene, provide pages of backstory, or describe characters' internal dilemmas, but in all probability, all you'll do is bore your readers. The best approach is to add in snippets of description or backstory, and only if they're needed, to clarify or illuminate the current situation. Internal dilemmas should be evident, not described.

As you read the following brief excerpt from my novel *Blood Rubies*, you'll notice the women's backstories are revealed solely through dialogue. Each revelation requires only three sentences. Josie's three sentences total thirty-eight words (38 words ÷ 3 sentences = an average of less than 13), while Ana's three sentences total twenty-seven words (27 words ÷ 3 sentences = an average of 9).

> I stood with Ana by the ocean, waiting for Ray to come get her.
>
> "Did you tell Peter about the mineral oil?" I asked.
>
> She didn't reply. She didn't look at me. Her gaze was steady on the ocean. The water had turned a dull dark green.
>
> "I mentioned it to you, and you told him, right? Not for a bad reason, just because it was an interesting little detail."
>
> She still didn't comment. I turned toward the water. Rows of striated waves thundered to shore fueled by a steady northeast wind.
>
> "I'm all alone," she said. "My husband left me for an older woman."
>
> "I'm sorry," I said.
>
> "I loved him, and he left me for a woman old enough to be his mother."
>
> "I had a boyfriend leave me because I was a downer, his word. I'd lost my job, my friends, and then my dad died, all within the space of a month or so. Two weeks later, he walked."
>
> "How did you cope?" Ana asked.
>
> "I moved to New Hampshire to start a new life."
>
> "Did it work?"
>
> "Yes."
>
> "Maybe there's hope for me."
>
> "Is there something I can do?" I asked.
>
> "No."
>
> I kept my eyes on the ocean. Neither of us spoke again until Ray pulled into the lot and Ana hurled herself into his arms.

FLASHBACKS

Flashbacks (discussed in chapter two as a versatile structural tool) can also be an effective technique to introduce backstory, but only if you simultaneously move the current story forward. Otherwise, they'll strike readers as irrelevant or a distraction. To use this approach effectively, you need to do the following:

1. Integrate the shift in time clearly.
2. Show why or how the backstory relates to the current story.
3. Keep it short.

You'll recall from Figure 2.1, the narrative question driving Al's memoir (Case Study #2): Will Al be able to continue meeting the needs of the people he loves: his wife, Mary, a banker; his dad, Hamilton, a retired lawyer; his sister, Kathy, a software company executive; and his rebellious teenage son, Stewart? As you read the example below, note how:

- The first few sentences set the scene, introduce the time shift, and justify including the memory (72 words ÷ 15 sentences = an average sentence length of less than 5).
- The last few sentences signal that we're back in the present time (54 words ÷ 5 sentences = an average sentence length of about 11).
- The entire scene is only 273 words long (with thirty-seven sentences, which gives us an average sentence length of less than eight words).

"Your mother called," Mary said. "She wants to come to Thanksgiving."

I stopped mashing the potatoes. "Dad'll have a stroke."

"He said it was fine."

"He's lying."

"She's retired."

"Lawyers never retire." I picked up the masher and resumed my slow pummeling. "Only mothers do."

I shut my eyes, willing myself to exorcise the memory. It didn't work. It never does. I was back in the kitchen with my mother. I was eight.

"Put the butter in first," my mother told me.

Dad charged into the kitchen and pinned mom with a glare cold enough to freeze the sun. "Who's Dave?" he bellowed.

I jumped, then stumbled, tripping over an untied shoelace.

His hand trembled as he held out a sheet of pale gray paper.

Mom glanced at it, then raised her eyes to his. She shrugged and turned back to the potatoes. "You're going through my drawers?"

"Answer me, you whore!"

She didn't speak. I backed away, one step at a time, holding my breath, until I ran into the refrigerator. I stayed still, wishing I could blink my eyes and disappear.

"Get out," he told her, his voice barely audible.

"With pleasure," she said, slamming the potato masher onto the counter. She washed her hands and dried them on a linen cloth. She smiled at me. "Bye, Al."

"What are you going to do, Al?" Mary asked, jolting me back to the here and now.

I opened my eyes as the ugly memory retreated. The past shackles you as surely as a ball and chain.

I grinned. "I'll do what I always do—handle whatever comes with a joke and a smile."

SHORTEN SENTENCES TO ADD TENSION

During moments of heightened tension, shorten sentences. Consider this sentence:

> From my vantage point in the storage closet, with the door open an inch, maybe less, I saw two men with guns wearing black ski masks enter the office and spin in opposite directions, one turning left while the other man turned right, scaring Melissa and Karl, so I sunk to my knees, praying they wouldn't find me.

That fifty-eight-word sentence communicates a boatload of information, but no tension. Look what happens if I take the same content, add more sensory references and active verbs, and shorten sentences:

> The office door burst open and two men wearing ski masks bolted in. I gasped and froze, stepping farther back into the musty storage closet. From the one-inch gap between the door and the frame, I watched them fan out. Melissa whimpered. Karl started to stand, then sank back into his chair. My mouth went dry. My hands curled

into fists. Guns. Each man held a gun, black with a silvery strip along the side. As they moved, flicks of light glinted off the metal. They screamed something I couldn't make out. I dropped to my knees and crawled along the knotty hardwood floor, wedging myself behind an old box of file folders, praying they wouldn't find me.

This 119-word paragraph is more than twice as long as the first draft. But it contains thirteen sentences, giving us an average sentence length of less than ten words, a dramatic difference and a vast improvement. By shortening sentences and adding language that enables readers to experience what the narrator is feeling, seeing, hearing, and thinking, in real time, readers perceive an urgency that the overly long run-on sentence failed to convey.

THREE TIPS FOR WRITING PERFECT SENTENCES

KNOW WHAT YOU WANT TO SAY BEFORE YOU PUT PEN TO PAPER. The more prewriting you do, the smoother your actual writing will be. Remember that each sentence needs to move the story along. Just as we discussed writing from TRD to TRD (see Jane's Plotting Road Map), so too should you write sentences that take readers from point to point.

INTEGRATE BOTH FACTS AND EMOTION. The best sentences include both information and how someone feels about that information. Use the journalist's five Ws (*who, what, when, where, why*, and perhaps, *how*) to determine which facts will propel your story forward. Focus on hot emotions like rage, devotion, despair, and loathing rather than lukewarm ones like happiness, annoyance, or sadness. As the great spy novelist John le Carré once said, "The cat sat on the mat is not a story. The cat sat on the other cat's mat is a story." As you write it up, tell us what the cat did to take possession of the other cat's mat. Why did he do it? Was he longing for that particular mat? Or was he simply looking for a way to twitch the other cat's tail? Marrying relevant facts to strong emotions leads to conflict and yearning, and conflict and yearning are the heart of effective storytelling.

MANAGE SENTENCE LENGTH, CADENCE, AND RHYTHM. Aim for an average sentence length of fewer than twenty words, varying lengths based on your objectives. Avoid unneeded modifiers like *very*, *really*, and *totally*, and use stronger nouns and verbs instead. Select words that precisely express your ideas. Challenge yourself to avoid all forms of the verb *to be* and labeling words. Add figures of speech like metaphors.

Note that the goal isn't merely to shorten sentences. You need to bring your setting to life. You need to ensure readers see and hear what the narrators see and hear. You need to add emotion by describing visceral reactions. Communicating on multiple levels helps add luster to your work.

The following excerpt from chapter nine of Sheila York's 2014 mystery, *No Broken Hearts*, for example, reveals information about the setting, the plot, and the protagonist. Set in the 1940s during Hollywood's Golden Age, the author's use of sensory references heightens the tension and drama. Notice how the spare dialogue and unusual sentence construction work together to illuminate a world of hurt.

> I walked along the path in the dim light cast by the moon. As I approached the base of the cabana steps, I saw wet shoe prints on the pale gray paving, coming toward me. I wouldn't have thought the grass was that wet. The gardener must have watered the lawn.
>
> The shoeprints turned before they reached me and headed up the steps, onto the glossy white paint. They continued into the lamplight.
>
> They were wet. But not from water.
>
> I heard a moan, low, agonized.
>
> "Roland?"
>
> I followed the prints to the door, edged my fingers forward, pushed it fully open.
>
> Roland Neale sat in a rattan chair, bent forward, his fists pressed to his face. His breathing was shallow, suffering. There was blood on the floor, not full prints anymore, but smeared bits across the painted planks. They led right to his feet, to the stained soles of his shoes.
>
> "Roland?"
>
> His head jerked up; he stared at me without comprehension.
>
> "It's Lauren," I said softly.
>
> "I would never have hurt her. Never."

"Who else is here?"

"I would never have hurt her."

"Of course not."

I took a step back and out onto the porch. The shoeprints were stark on the white planks. They came from the opposite direction I had, from the other end of the cabana. I forced myself along the porch to the far railing, looked over. The paving became a small patio, dotted with flowering plants in large wooden pots. A woman lay crumpled on her side between two of them. I could see a bit of the blue hem of her dress, her slender legs, and her black evening shoes, their soles facing me, with their narrow diamanté straps.

I staggered back, dropping my bag, my hands over my mouth. I fell against the cabana wall, caught the sill of the window, steadied myself. I had to get out of here. Now. Go back to the lane. Back to the Brackers' and people. And safety.

Move. Run.

I rounded the corner. And collided with the tall, hard shape of a man.

He grabbed my arm. I punched him hard in the face. He whipped me around, threw one hand over my mouth and the other around my waist. He dragged me back into the cabana and kicked the door shut.

LET YOUR VOICE SHINE THROUGH

Whether you're writing a sweeping family saga, a dystopian novel, a thriller, a children's book, or a memoir; whether your book is plot driven or character driven, you want to make sure your work sounds like you. This is harder than it sounds. No matter how hard you've worked or how fabulous your ideas, if your sentences sound ordinary, clunky, stock, run-on, mechanical, or awkward, readers won't be able to see how your work differs from everyone else's. One of the most common reasons books don't get published is that they lack a distinctive voice.

FAQ

Q: I read a lot and always have. I reread my favorites, too, and sometimes I find myself writing with the cadence of *their* sentences. It's not that I'm trying to mimic them—it's that the rhythm becomes fixed in my head. How do I know whether my writer's voice is derivative or not? And if it is, how do I find my own?

A: You raise an important question. In my experience, many authors quash their unique voice. Usually this reflects their fear that if they let it all hang out, they'll ultimately have to confront the reality that readers don't warm to their efforts. They fret they'll be teased or mocked or summarily rejected. They pull their punches so they won't have to take flack or be hurt. This fear of failure can be debilitating. It's a common cause of writer's block, and even if you power through the block, you end up writing bland nothings rather than sharp-edged insights.

You'll recall we spent a significant amount of time analyzing what your specific readers like and expect and want (see chapter one). Put this information to work! Try this two-part exercise:

1. **CREATE AN IMAGINARY FRIEND, AN IDEALIZED READER**, someone who, based on the research and analysis you did in chapter one, loves your genre. You know you don't have to worry that this person will ding you in any way. He's on your side. He wants you to succeed. He's patient and kind. Write with abandon to that particular person. Some find it helpful to record a pretend conversation with this reader, transcribe the recording and then use the transcription as their first draft. Don't edit yourself as you're writing (or speaking). That's a separate step that will come later. Try to write a paragraph, a page, or a short scene that sounds like you dream you can write. The old saying "Fake it till you make it" applies here. Write as if the words flow, and they'll flow. Remember, your imaginary friend is actually imaginary—no one but you will ever see this draft, so go for it. Revise it. Revise it again.

2. **SELECT A FAVORITE EXAMPLE FROM YOUR GENRE.** (When I did this exercise before writing my first Josie Prescott Antiques Mystery, I picked Dick Francis's first-person traditional mystery, *Reflex*. I chose it because it was in the same genre as I wanted to

write, and I loved it.) Compare your work to your selection using specific metrics, such as average sentence length, use of the word *I* (a crucial barometer in writing first-person stories that are nonetheless reader focused), use of any form of the verb "to be," and any other modes of assessment you deem appropriate. See where you diverge from the book you're modeling on. Does anything you did smack of a pastiche?

Once you're aware of what you've done well, keep doing it. Take those bits that you don't like and change them. The trick is to differentiate between creating and critiquing. If you're struggling with letting your own special voice into the world, you're probably trying to do both steps at once. Separating them is liberating! First write, then, as a separate step, assess your work.

Your writer's voice is an amalgam of your thoughts, beliefs, feelings, observations, and intuitions expressed in a nonderivative way. Whether it's cadence, word choice, phrasing, use of dialect, all of these, or none of these, or something else all together, your work needs to *sound* like you. Write raw. Write bareback. Don't go tame. Write the truth. People are hungry for the truth. Write it, and they will come. In fact, they'll probably beat a path to your door.

WRITE PURPOSEFULLY

As you try your hand at revising the overly long, confusing, and ordinary sentence in Figure 13.1, don't forget to add your individual spin so the revision sounds like you. Then, after you revise the sentence, consider where you took this challenge. Did you focus on the work aspect of the situation, or did you jettison work for love? Did you think about character, plot, setting, and mood and then focus on the words themselves? How about voice? Were you able to write with abandon so that the excerpt sounds like you?

FIGURE 13.1: REVISE PURPOSEFULLY

Before revising this sentence, decide what you want to express. What facts do you want to include? What emotions?

MASTERING SUSPENSE, STRUCTURE, & PLOT

If you're like most writers, you've learned that it's easier to write when you know what you want to express. The lesson is to think first, then write, then revise. And don't forget: Words matter. Which brings us to our last task—pulling it all together.

CHAPTER FOURTEEN

CONCLUSION

66 Whatever is hidden behind the curtain must be revealed at last, 99 and it must be at one and the same time completely unexpected and inevitable.

—MARGARET ATWOOD

END WITH FORETHOUGHT: THE TRIPLE X STRATEGY

By the end of the story, all primary and secondary plotlines have to be addressed, all character questions have to be answered, all conflicts have to be resolved, and you have to do it without relying on coincidence or contrivance. In order to accomplish this, you need to track plot and character details, which can be an organizational challenge. My Triple X Strategy will help you manage the process.

STEP ONE: Anytime that your book mentions an issue that you know you need to resolve at some point in the future, or if you're unhappy with something you've written, type "xxx." Since "xxx" doesn't appear in any word in English, you can easily search for it (using control F in Word) and address each occurrence one at a time when you're ready.

STEP TWO: Either at the bottom of your manuscript or in a separate document, create a list of "plot threads." Periodically review the list to keep them in your consciousness. This way, you won't risk forgetting to address them.

Here are two examples from Case Study #1 (the domestic thriller) of how the Triple X Strategy can help you write cohesive stories.

- On page 5, I mention that Kayla loves shrimp, but she can't eat them because she's allergic. If I don't bring up the shrimp again, I will have committed a Chekhov's gun error (see chapter one), but I don't want to have to rely on my memory to loop back to that initial reference. My solution: I type "xxx" next to the word *shrimp*, then go to my plot thread list and add "Kayla—shrimp allergy" to the list. Note: Don't reference the specific page number because they'll invariably change as you revise.

- On page 20, I write a sentence I don't like. I know I want to think about it more and rework the passage, but I don't want to get bogged down with it while I'm getting my initial ideas down on paper. My solution: I type "xxx" at the beginning of the sentence.

The Triple X Strategy frees you from the onus of having to keep too many details in your head. When your brain is not cluttered, you can write in the here and now with total focus.

FAQ

Q: Do the lessons in this book apply to short stories, too?

A: Yes. No matter the scope of the story you want to tell, you still need a narrative question, TRDs, character development, elegant prose, and a slow reveal, and as such, all the tools discussed in this book work for short stories. Here are two additional tips from Linda Landrigan, editor-in-chief of *Alfred Hitchcock's Mystery Magazine*:

1. The concept of the "telling detail" is important, especially in short stories where space is at a premium. The spot-on detail can evoke a whole scene in your readers' imagination. One efficient technique to boost suspense is to include a disharmonious detail—the off-note that suggests all is not right with the scene before you.
2. Some writers feel that the technique of the slow reveal doesn't apply in short stories simply because of the brevity of the work, but they are mistaken. The manner in which important details are revealed has everything to do with the overall narrative pacing of the story. It is the method by which you build narrative momentum.

No matter what kinds of stories you want to tell, these suggestions will help you add panache—and suspense—to your work.

However you track your work-in-progress, remember that your most important goal is to tell the story you want to tell and to do so with passion and clarity. With passion and clarity comes illumination, and with illumination comes acclaim.

ILLUMINATE THE WAY AND READERS WILL STEP INTO YOUR WORLD

When Arthur Miller, the great playwright, was president of PEN (PEN stands for poets, playwrights, essayists, editors, and novelists), he wrote, "PEN is the voice of cultures truthfully addressing one another rather than governments or armies in confrontation. The object is not to win something, but to illuminate something." Illuminate—a carefully chosen word to describe a lofty writing challenge—find ways to express the truth while keeping your readers on the edge of their seats.

Your job as a writer is to open the door and invite your readers in, to allow them to share in your characters' experiences. Let your readers in. Don't thrust them in. Don't drag them in. People are smart. Readers are smart. And in general, people only do what they want to do, which means that to persuade, educate, and entertain, you must entice, seduce, and reveal, not bludgeon. You must, as Arthur Miller expressed it, illuminate.

PUT THE TOOLS TO WORK

Your character is in trouble. Danger looms. It's tempting to explain the experience, to talk about what your character believes or thinks, but it's far more gripping to let your readers feel what your character feels, in real time. For instance, instead of writing "Tommy realized his brother was missing," try:

> Tommy saw Jake's baseball glove sitting in its usual place, on top of the old bureau. The weak winter sun hit the rubbed spot on the left side of the mitt, the place where Jake had snagged a hundred line drives, a thousand. Tommy's eyes filled, and he brushed the wetness away with a rough, angry swipe of the side of his hand. He coughed as his throat clenched. Jake would never leave his glove behind. Never.

Isn't it better? Can you feel the tension? Can you feel Tommy's dread? Don't you want to know where Jake is?

You can write with this kind of passion and clarity, too. Use the checklist in Figure 14.1 to guide you through the writing process and to make sure you haven't forgotten anything. It can also help you overcome writer's block by narrowing the scope of your work—you don't need to take on an entire project. All you need to do is address one question at a time.

FIGURE 14.1: WRITING CHECKLIST

- Have you analyzed the exemplars of your chosen genre? What did you learn that you can apply to your own work?

- What structure did you choose, linear or nonlinear? Should you use any enhancements, such as bookends, categories, flashbacks or flash-forwards?

- What is your narrative question?

- Have you plotted your novel (or delineated your story line, if you're writing a memoir or literary nonfiction)?

- Do you know what drives your character to act? List a few salient facts about your character that direct his or her action—have you sufficiently integrated them?

- What do you know about your setting? What makes it special? What makes it worth writing about? How does it inform your character? How does it inform your plot?

- Have you selected two subplots?

- Have you integrated enough TRDs?

- Have you used weak "in-your-head" words like *realize* and *know*?

- Have you used any form of the verb *to be* (*is, are, was, were, be, being, been*)? If so, can/should you revise the sentence to include an active verb? (Note: While not every usage of *to be* is inappropriate, do challenge yourself to evaluate whether an active verbs would make the sentence stronger.)

- Can you add metaphors?

- Are you using red herrings? Are they well planted?

- Are you foreshadowing moments of danger? Should you?

- Have you integrated any surprises? Have you developed them into suspenseful moments by more fully informing your readers about the situation or some aspect of the situation?

- Have you added specificity through sensory references? Have you used sensory references to eliminate moments of "telling"?

- Who has betrayed your character? Why?

- How is your character coping with that betrayal?

- What are the stakes? What are the consequences of your characters failing at whatever goals you've assigned them? Are they high enough?

- Have you set up slow reveals?

- By the end of your book, have you answered your narrative question?

- What's your average sentence length? Is it low enough?

- Are you using a variety of sentence lengths?

- Does coincidence figure in anywhere in your story? If so, you need to eliminate it—go back to the beginning and plant facts, create incidents, or change a character attribute so what feels contrived now, is, as Margaret Atwood put it, "unexpected and inevitable."

- Have you thought about the words you've chosen? Is each word precise?

- Are you repeating words too often? Do you have "favorites" or pet words you tend to use over and over again? Search for them and replace them, as needed.

- Have all your plot threads come together seamlessly?

- Have you expressed yourself uninhibitedly? Are you writing with an unfettered voice?

- Does your story end with a global reflection?

If, as you review the items listed in Figure 14.1, you find anything unclear, or if you want to think more about a particular issue, go back to those sections in the book that correspond with your questions. Reread the examples, then adapt the principles to your work. Experiment!

THINK, WRITE, REVISE (IN THAT ORDER)

As you work through this final exercise (Figure 14.2), remember that there are countless ways to express any one idea—don't feel as if you're on a hunt for a single "right" approach. Here are some tips for successful role-playing:

- Picture the scene.
- Look at the characters in your mind's eye.
- Anticipate the action.
- Place yourself in that moment, then write up the scene with confidence.
- Let your unique writer's voice resonate as you draft your revision.
- Trust the process.

FIGURE 14.2: EXERCISE: PULL THE TOOLS TOGETHER

PART ONE: Role-play to create a situation in which Marney, finding herself alone, is frightened—or in which she is frightening. Consider how you might add sensory details as you replace the word *knew* in the following sentence: *Marney knew she wasn't alone.*

- Describe what Marney sees that makes her know she isn't alone.
- Describe what Marney hears that makes her know she isn't alone.
- What is Marney touching? How does it feel against her skin?
- When Marney swallows, how does it feel? What taste is in her mouth?
- Is there an aroma? A scent? A stink? Describe it.

PART TWO: Using one or more of your sensory observations, revise the example to add urgency and specificity. Draw your readers in and make the moment leap off the page.

- Where are you taking this? Write your revision now.

SUMMARIZE AND REFLECT:

- What is your assessment of your work?
- Did this methodical process help you produce more robust work?
- What are the key takeaways that you want to remember and use in your writing going forward?
- What will you do differently next time?

MASTERING SUSPENSE, STRUCTURE, & PLOT

FINAL THOUGHTS

Remember, structure is king. Clarity is queen. Character and incident must walk together in lockstep. Sensory allusions carry the day by helping you show, not tell. Avoid exposition. As much as possible, tell your story using dialogue and action scenes. Confirm you've answered the narrative question. Polish your language. Choose words wisely. Add metaphors.

And as you write and reflect on your work when it's done, remember to be gentle with yourself. Writing is hard. Revising is hard. But applying these tools will ensure your stories resonate with readers. They will find good publishing homes. They will sell. And they will be loved.

AFTERWORD

THE VALUES OF WRITING

Value #1: Honor Your Readers

My mother was born in 1910. She died nearly twenty years ago. I would not be a writer if I were not my mother's daughter. She was a writer, and she considered it a calling. She wrote all sorts of things, including scores of those anonymous, racy first-person stories that were published in magazines like *True Romance* in the mid-twentieth century.

> I was twelve when I stumbled on a cardboard box in the attic filled with my mother's manuscripts. The first one I picked up was entitled, "I Knew He Was Married, but I Didn't Care. I Was, Too." I fell back on my haunches. Sitting there alone, I read it, then I read it again, and then I marched downstairs and demanded an explanation.
>
> "Ma," I said, my disapproval patent, "what's this?"
>
> She glanced at the manuscript. "That's the new stove."

Value number one: Write to please your readers, and when you do it well, your work will sell, it will be read, and readers will want more. Write for your readers, not yourself.

Value #2: Be Patient

My mother liked revision better than writing. Me too. With revision, you get to think of the right structure, the right words, the right cadence of the language, and the emotions you want to convey. Don't be in a hurry. Don't fall in love with your writing—that's the equivalent of falling in love with love, not the person. Revise with an eagle's eye, an objective view, and a clear understanding of your readers' expectations.

Each author must develop his or her own writing process. Here's mine: I use a very specific three-step approach. I lay down plot; I revise to integrate emotion, character motivation, and sensory references; and I revise over and over again until I get the words right.

Ernest Hemingway once told F. Scott Fitzgerald, "I write one page of masterpiece to ninety-one pages of shit. I try to put the shit in the wastebasket."

Value number two: Don't expect your first drafts to be your final drafts.

Value #3: Embrace Your Own Values

My mother valued the truth above all else. She was of the "leave nothing unsaid" school of communication, and that's what she did all the time. It made her hard to be around sometimes, and lonely a lot of the time, since many people didn't share her reverence for the truth. But it also made her absolutely trustworthy. You always knew where you stood with her.

Value number three: Know what you value. Write that.

Value #4: Be Kind to Yourself

The path to becoming a published author is twisty and filled with obstacles. Following the twists and overcoming the obstacles is part of the process—there is no shortcut, or if there is one,

I don't know it. Writers need to learn the craft of writing. We each need to find our unique voice. We need to find the courage to send our work out into the marketplace. Yes, writing requires discipline. But it also requires self-kindness.

Value number four: Be kind to yourself.

Four values that, taken together, form a writer's manifesto. Be bold, be generous, be focused, and be self-reliant. Write like you mean it.

I have absolute confidence that you can do these things, and that you can do them well.

I believe in you.

INDEX

MASTERING SUSPENSE, STRUCTURE, & PLOT

grammar, conversational, 201–2
Guest, Judith, 61–62
guilt, 189–90
Gun with Wings, The (Stout), 109–10

halo effect, 104–6
Hawkins, Paula, 121, 136–37, 190
hearing, 159
Heyer, Georgette, 16–17, 40
historical fiction, 60
historical romance, 16–17, 40
Holding, Elisabeth Sanxay, 63
human nature, 100–102, 103, 106
Hunger Games trilogy, 80

"I Gotta Tell You" (Seeger), 11
Iacocca, Lee, 11
ideas, finding, 39–43
ignorance, 104
impending doom, sense of, 31
incident-driven decision making, 53–55
inciting incident, 32, 38, 67
information flow, 29
inner turmoil, 136–37
innocence, 112, 188–89
isolation, 82–89
    and characterizations, 89–91
    and loneliness, 91–92
    and metaphors, 93–99
    and plot, 84–86
It (King), 125–26

jack-in-the-box effect, 114–20
Jane's Plotting Road Map, 35–52, 70, 76–79
Josie Prescott series (Cleland), 8, 26
    bookends, 27
    plotting, 39–40, 42
    red herrings, 109
    subplots, 75, 80, 81
    surprise, 116–20
    theme, 68
    TRDs, 55
    using small sounds to increase tension, 156–57

Kesey, Ken, 190–91
Killer Keepsakes (Cleland), 55, 75
King, Stephen, 125–26
Kluger, Jeffrey, 173
knowledge gaps, 146–52

language, 160–71
Larry's Kidney (Rose), 41
Last Saxon, The (O'Donnell), 45
Lehane, Dennis, 57
leisurely pace, 44
Lethal Treasure (Cleland), 116–20
Light, Lawrence, 204
linear structure, 20, 21
literary fiction, 11, 40–41, 63, 74–75
literary journalism, 12
literary nonfiction, 11–12
logic flaws, 104
London Eye Mystery, The (Dowd), 41
loneliness, 91–92
longing, character's, 12, 59, 61, 186
Lord of the Ring series, 75

MacDonald, John D., 79–80
Mahmoody, Betty, 62–63
McBain, Ed, 198
"Mean Yellow Jacket" (Peters), 193–97
memoir, 12. *See also* Case Study #2
    and isolation, 89–91
    pacing, 51
    plotting, 41, 42–43
    and sensual references, 65–66
    setting, 62–63
    and structure, 32–34
    and subplots, 73, 75, 78
memory, 188
mental illness, 190–91
Metaphor Machine, 94–99
metaphors, 93–99, 164–65
middle school mystery, 41
Munier, Paula, 93–94
"Murder at an Ad Agency" (Anthony), 186–87
Murder Notebook, The (Santlofer), 146
Murder of Roger Ackroyd, The (Christie), 110, 190
"Muse of the Coyote Ugly Saloon" (Gilbert), 27–28
My Faith So Far (Dodd), 137–38
My Sister's Keeper (Picoult), 121
mysteries, traditional. *See* traditional mysteries

narrative flow, 24, 31
narrative journalism, 12
narrative nonfiction, 11–12
narrative question, 15–16, 49, 102, 186, 206
narrator
    omniscient, 25–26, 30
    unreliable, 116, 187–91

MASTERING SUSPENSE, STRUCTURE, & PLOT